From
Magna Carta
to the
Constitution

Documents in the Struggle for Liberty

Edited by David L. Brooks

Fox &
Wilkes

Published by Fox & Wilkes
942 Howard Street, San Francisco, CA 94103

Printed in the United States of America
ISBN 0-930073-07-X

Table of Contents

Preface

When John Dickinson stood up in the Constitutional Convention and declared that "Experience must be our only guide," he was not speaking of his personal experience, or even the experience of those at the Convention as a whole, great though it was: various members of the Convention had served in Continental Congresses, signed the Declaration of Independence, served in the legislatures of the various States and in the Confederation Congress. But they also possessed a different kind of experience. They had read their history, and they knew the kinds of innovations by which people had attempted to control the powers of government and secure their liberties. Their experience here was vast, for they had more than seven centuries of British history alone to draw on, as well as that of the Ancients.

This little book is a selection of ten British and American documents that embodied the ideas the Founders looked to in their effort to frame a government of limited powers. If it is true that to understand the present we must study the past, it is also true that to understand the Constitution, how it was and how it is, how it succeeded and how it failed, we must understand the history of the ideas that went into it.

This book sketches part of that history; a very small part, but not an unimportant part. The problems of government are with us still. And if we are to make changes for the better today, we need to understand the changes attempted yesterday.

The editor would like to thank Mr. Len Kahn for his generous assistance and helpful suggestions. Spelling and capitalization have sometimes been changed to reflect modern usage for ease of reading.

The feudal relationship between the king and his barons involved the king granting titles, lands, revenues and rights in return for service, usually military service. King John's barons thought that he had broken the feudal contract by usurping the lands, rights and revenues that belonged to them, and they rebelled and forced him to confirm the feudal contract and foreswear his usurpations. The barons were faced with the perennial problem: how to limit the power of the king and government. They adopted the method of declaring that the king was bound by the law, as were all citizens, and they attempted to bind and limit the king through a written instrument. Two specific ideas to note in Magna Carta are both found in Chapter 39: the right of trial by jury, which would play an immense role in limiting the power of government, and the notion of "the law of the land," which, in a later confirmation of the Charter, became "due process of law," a pregnant phrase in American jurisprudence. Magna Carta well deserves the title of "The Great Charter of English Liberties."

Magna Carta
(1215)

(From *Selected Historical Documents of the Middle Ages*, as translated by Ernest F. Henderson)

John, by the grace of God king of England, lord of Ireland, duke of Normandy and Aquitaine, count of Anjou: to the archbishops, bishops, abbots, earls, barons, justices, foresters, sheriffs, prevosts, serving men, and to all his bailiffs and faithful subjects, greeting. Know that we, by the will of God and for the safety of our soul, and of the souls of all our predecessors and our heirs, to the honor of God and for the exalting of our holy church and the bettering of our realm: by the counsel of our venerable fathers Stephen archbishop of Canterbury, primate of all England and cardinal of the holy Roman church; of Henry archbishop of Dublin; of the bishops William of London, Peter of Winchester, Jocelin of Bath and Glaston-bury, Hugo of Lincoln, Walter of Worcester, William of Coventry and Benedict of Rochester; of master Pandulf, subdeacon and of the household of the lord pope; of brother Aymeric master of the knights of the Temple in England; and of the noble men, William Marshall earl of Pembroke, William earl of Salisbury, William earl of Warren, William earl of Arundel, Alan de Galway constable of Scotland, Warin son of Gerold, Peter son of Herbert, Hubert de Burgh seneschal of Poictiers, Hugo de Neville, Matthew son of Herbert, Thomas Basset, Alan Basset, Philip d'Aubigni, Robert de Roppelay, John Marshall, John son of Hugo, and others of our faithful subjects:

1. First of all have granted to God, and, for us and for our heirs forever, have confirmed, by this our present charter, that the English church shall be free and shall have its rights intact and its liberties uninfringed upon. And thus we will that it be observed. As is apparent from the fact that we, spontaneously and of our own free will, before discord broke out between ourselves and our barons, did grant and by our charter confirm—and did cause the lord pope Innocent III, to confirm—freedom of elections, which is considered most important and most necessary to the church of England. Which charter both we ourselves shall observe, and we will that it be observed with good faith by our heirs forever. We have also granted to all free men of our realm, on the part of ourselves and our heirs forever, all the subjoined liberties, to have and to hold, to them and their heirs, from us and from our heirs:

2. If any one of our earls or barons, or of others holding from us in chief through military service, shall die; and if, at the time of his death, his heir be of full age and owe a relief:[1] he shall have his inheritance by paying the old relief;—the heir, namely, or the heirs of an earl, by paying one hundred pounds for the whole barony of an earl; the heir or heirs of a baron, by paying one hundred pounds for the whole barony; the heir or heirs of a knight, by paying one hundred shillings

---

1. Payment made by the heir of a vassal to the lord on inheritance of an estate.

at most for a whole knight's fee; and he who shall owe less shall give less, according to the ancient custom of fees.

3. But if the heir of any of the above persons shall be under age and in wardship,—when he comes of age he shall have his inheritance without relief and without fine.

4. The administrator of the land of such heir who shall be under age shall take none but reasonable issues from the land of the heir, and reasonable customs and services; and this without destruction and waste of men or goods. And if we shall have committed the custody of any such land to the sheriff or to any other man who ought to be responsible to us for the issues of it, and he cause destruction or waste to what is in his care: we will fine him, and the land shall be handed over to two lawful and discreet men of that fee[2] who shall answer to us, or to him to whom we shall have referred them, regarding those issues. And if we shall have given or sold to any one the custody of any such land, and he shall have caused destruction or waste to it,—he shall lose that custody, and it shall be given to two lawful and discreet men of that fee, who likewise shall answer to us, as has been explained.

5. The administrator, moreover, so long as he may have the custody of the land, shall keep in order, from the issues of that land, the houses, parks, warrens, lakes, mills, and other things pertaining to it. And he shall restore to the heir when he comes to full age, his whole land stocked with ploughs and wainnages,[3] according as the time of the wainnage requires and the issues of the land will reasonably permit.

6. Heirs may marry without disparagement; so, nevertheless, that, before the marriage is contracted, it shall be announced to the relations by blood of the heir himself.

7. A widow, after the death of her husband, shall straightway, and without difficulty, have her marriage portion and her inheritance, nor shall she give any thing in return for her dowry, her marriage portion, or the inheritance which be-

---

2. A fief or estate.
3. Agricultural implements and animals necessary to tillage.

longed to her, and which she and her husband held on the day of the death of that husband. And she may remain in the house of her husband, after his death, for forty days; within which her dowry shall be paid over to her.

8. No widow shall be forced to marry when she prefers to live without a husband; so, however, that she gives security not to marry without our consent, if she hold from us, or the consent of the lord from whom she holds, if she hold from another.

9. Neither we nor our bailiffs shall seize any revenue for any debt, so long as the chattels of the debtor suffice to pay the debt; nor shall the sponsors of that debtor be distrained so long as the chief debtor has enough to pay the debt. But if the chief debtor fail in paying the debt, not having the where-withal to pay it, the sponsors shall answer for the debt. And, if they shall wish, they may have the lands and revenues of the debtor until satisfaction shall have been given them for the debt previously paid for him; unless the chief debtor shall show that he is quit in that respect towards those same sponsors.

10. If any one shall have taken any sum, great or small, as a loan from the money-lenders, and shall die before that debt is paid,—that debt shall not bear interest so long as the heir, from whomever he may hold, shall be under age. And if the debt fall into our hands, we shall take nothing save the chattel contained in the deed.

11. And if any one dies owing a debt to the money-lenders, his wife shall have her dowry, and shall restore nothing of that debt. But if there shall remain children of that dead man, and they shall be under age, the necessaries shall be provided for them according to the nature of the dead man's holding; and, from the residue, the debt shall be paid, saving the service due to the lords. In like manner shall be done concerning debts that are due to others besides money-lenders.

12. No scutage[4] or aid shall be imposed in our realm unless by the common counsel of our realm; except for redeeming

---

4. Money paid by a vassal to his lord in lieu of personal service.

our body, and knighting our eldest son, and marrying once our eldest daughter. And for these purposes there shall only be given a reasonable aid. In like manner shall be done concerning the city of London.

13. And the city of London shall have all its old liberties and free customs as well by land as by water. Moreover we will grant that all other cities and burroughs, and towns and ports, shall have all their liberties and free customs.

14. And, in order to have common counsel of the realm in the matter of assessing an aid otherwise than in the aforesaid cases, or of assessing a scutage—we shall cause, under seal through our letters, the archbishops, bishops, abbots, earls, and greater barons to be summoned for a fixed day—for a term, namely, at least forty days distant,—and for a fixed place. And, moreover, we shall cause to be summoned in general, through our sheriffs and bailiffs, all those who hold of us in chief. And in all those letters of summons we shall express the cause of the summons. And when a summons has thus been made, the business shall be proceeded with on the day appointed according to the counsel of those who shall be present, even though not all shall come who were summoned.

15. We will not allow any one henceforth to take an aid from his freemen save for the redemption of his body, and the knighting of his eldest son, and the marrying, once, of his eldest daughter; and, for these purposes, there shall only be given a reasonable aid.

16. No one shall be forced to do more service for a knight's fee, or for another free holding, than is due from it.

17. Common pleas shall not follow our court but shall be held in a certain fixed place.

18. Assizes of novel disseisin, of mort d'ancestor, and of darrein presentment[5] shall not be held save in their own

---

5. An assize was a trial in which a sworn jury decided a question of fact. In these three possessory assizes the jury decided, respectively, whether the plaintiff had been ousted from an estate, whether the plaintiff was a close relative of one who had died in possession of the property in dispute, and whether the plaintiff, a clergyman, was in

counties, and in this way: We, or our chief justice, if we shall be absent from the kingdom, shall send two justices through each county four times a year; they, with four knights from each county, chosen by the county, shall hold the aforesaid assizes in the county, and on the day and at the place of the county court.

19. And if on the day of the county court the aforesaid assizes can not be held, a sufficient number of knights and free tenants, from those who were present at the county court on that day, shall remain, so that through them the judgments may be suitably given, according as the matter may have been great or small.

20. A freeman shall only be amerced for a small offence according to the measure of that offence. And for a great offence he shall be amerced according to the magnitude of the offence, saving his contenement;[6] and a merchant, in the same way, saving his merchandize. And a villein, in the same way, if he fall under our mercy, shall be amerced saving his wainnage. And none of the aforesaid fines shall be imposed save upon oath of upright men from the neighborhood.

21. Earls and barons shall not be amerced save through their peers, and only according to the measure of the offence.

22. No clerk shall be amerced for his lay tenement except according to the manner of the other persons aforesaid; and not according to the amount of his ecclesiastical benefice.

23. Neither a town nor a man shall be forced to make bridges over the rivers, with the exception of those who, from of old and of right ought to do it.

24. No sheriff, constable, coroners, or other bailiffs of ours shall hold the pleas of our crown.

25. All counties, hundreds, wapentakes, and trithings—our demesne manors[7] being excepted—shall continue according to the old farms, without any increase at all.

---

possession of an appointment, or presentment, to church livings.
6. The property of a freeman necessary for him to maintain his position.
7. Estates owned by the king, from which he was expected to maintain

26. If any one holding from us a lay fee shall die, and our sheriff or bailiff can show our letters patent containing our summons for the debt which the dead man owed us,—our sheriff or bailiff may be allowed to attach and enroll the chattels of the dead man to the value of that debt, through view of lawful men; in such way, however, that nothing shall be removed thence until the debt is paid which was plainly owed to us. And the residue shall be left to the executors that they may carry out the will of the dead man. And if nothing is owed to us by him, all the chattels shall go to the use prescribed by the deceased, saving their reasonable portions to his wife and children.

27. If any freeman shall have died intestate his chattels shall be distributed through the hands of his near relatives and friends, by view of the church; saving to any one the debts which the dead man owed him.

28. No constable or other bailiff of ours shall take the corn or other chattels of any one except he straightway give money for them, or can be allowed a respite in that regard by the will of the seller.

29. No constable shall force any knight to pay money for castleward if he be willing to perform that ward in person, or—he for a reasonable cause not being able to perform it himself—through another proper man. And if we shall have led or sent him on a military expedition, he shall be quit of ward according to the amount of time during which, through us, he shall have been in military service.

30. No sheriff nor bailiff of ours, nor any one else, shall take the horses or carts of any freeman for transport, unless by the will of that freeman.

31. Neither we nor our bailiffs shall take another's wood for castles or for other private uses, unless by the will of him to whom the wood belongs.

---

his household and pay all of the ordinary expenses of government.

32. We shall not hold the lands of those convicted of felony longer than a year and a day; and then the lands shall be restored to the lords of the fiefs.

33. Henceforth all weirs in the Thames and Medway, and throughout all England, save on the sea-coast, shall be done away with entirely.

34. Henceforth the writ which is called *Praecipe* shall not be served on any one for any holding so as to cause a free man to lose his court.

35. There shall be one measure of wine throughout our whole realm and one measure of ale and one measure of corn—namely, the London quart;—and one width of dyed and russet and hauberk cloths—namely, two ells below selvage. And with weights, moreover, it shall be as with measures.

36. Henceforth nothing shall be given or taken for a writ of inquest in a matter concerning life or limb; but it be conceded gratis, and shall not be denied.

37. If any one hold of us in fee-farm, or in socage, or in burkage,[8] and hold land of another by military service, we shall not, by reason of the fee-farm, or socage, or burkage, have the wardship of his heir or of his land which is held in fee from another. Nor shall we have the wardship of the fee-farm, or socage, or burkage unless that fee-farm owe military service. We shall not, by reason of some petit-serjeanty which some one holds of us through the service of giving us knives or arrows or the like, have the wardship of his heir or of the land which he holds of another by military service.

38. No bailiff, on his own simple assertion, shall henceforth put any one to his law, without producing faithful witnesses in evidence.

---

8. Land held in fee-farm was held from a lord on payment of a money rent; land held in socage was held from a lord for money payment and certain agricultural duties; and burkage was land held from a lord in a town or borough on payment of a money rent.

39. No freeman shall be taken, imprisoned, or disseized, or outlawed, or exiled, or in any way harmed—nor will we go upon or send upon him—save by the lawful judgment of his peers or by the law of the land.

40. To none will we sell, and none deny or delay, right or justice.

41. All merchants may safely and securely go out of England, and come into England, and delay and pass through England, as well by land as by water, for the purpose of buying and selling, free from all evil taxes, subject to the ancient and right customs—save in time of war, and if they are of the land at war against us. And if such be found in our land at the beginning of the war, they shall be held, without harm to their bodies and goods, until it shall be known to us or our chief justice how the merchants of our land are to be treated who shall, at that time, be found in the land at war against us. And if ours shall be safe there, the other shall be safe in our land.

42. Henceforth any person, saving fealty to us, may go out of our realm and return to it, safely and securely, by land and by water, except perhaps for a brief period in time of war, for the common good of the realm. But prisoners and outlaws are excepted according to the law of the realm; also people of a land at war against us, and the merchants, with regard to whom it shall be done as we have said.

43. If any one hold from any escheat[9]—as from the honor of Wallingford, Nottingham, Boloin, Lancaster, or the other escheats which are in our hands and are baronies—and shall die, his heir shall not give another relief, nor shall he perform for us other service than he would perform for a baron if that barony were in the hand of a baron; and we shall hold it in the same way in which the baron has held it.

44. Persons dwelling without the forest shall not henceforth come before the forest justices, through common sum-

---

9. Property that reverted to the Crown on the owner dying without legal heirs.

monses, unless they are impleaded or are the sponsors of some person or persons attached for matters concerning the forest.

45. We will not make men justices, constables, sheriffs, or bailiffs, unless they are such as know the law of the realm, and are minded to observe it rightly.

46. All barons who have founded abbeys for which they have charters of the kings of England, or ancient right of tenure, shall have, as they ought to have, their custody when vacant.

47. All forests constituted as such in our time shall straightway be annulled; and the same shall be done for river banks made into places of defence by us in our time.

48. All evil customs concerning forests and warrens, and concerning foresters and warreners, sheriffs and their servants, river banks and their guardians, shall straightway be inquired into in each county, through twelve sworn knights from that county, and shall be eradicated by them, entirely, so that they shall never be renewed, within forty days after the inquest has been made; in such manner that we shall first know about them, or our justice if we be not in England.

49. We shall straightway return all hostages and charters which were delivered to us by Englishmen as a surety for peace or faithful service.

50. We shall entirely remove from their bailwicks the relatives of Gerard de Athyes, so that they shall henceforth have no bailwick in England: Engelard de Cygnes, Andrew Peter and Gyon de Chanceles, Gyon de Cygnes, Geoffrey de Martin and his brothers, Philip Mark and his brothers, and Geoffrey his nephew, and the whole following of them.

51. And straightway after peace is restored we shall remove from the realm all the foreign soldiers, crossbowmen, servants, hirelings, who may have come with horses and arms to the harm of the realm.

52. If any one shall have been disseized by us, or removed, without a legal sentence of his peers, from his lands, castles, liberties or lawful right, we shall straightway restore them to him. And if a dispute shall arise concerning this matter it shall be settled according to the judgment of the twenty five barons

who are mentioned below as sureties for the peace. But with regard to all those things of which any one was, by king Henry our father or king Richard our brother, disseized or dispossessed without legal judgment of his peers, which we have in our hand or which others hold, and for which we ought to give a guarantee: We shall have respite until the common term for crusaders. Except with regard to those concerning which a plea was moved, or an inquest made by our order, before we took the cross. But when we return from our pilgrimage, or if, by chance, we desist from our pilgrimage, we shall straightway then show full justice regarding them.

53. We shall have the same respite, moveover, and in the same manner, in the matter of showing justice with regard to forests to be annulled and forests to remain, which Henry our father or Richard our brother constituted; and in the matter of wardships of lands which belong to the fee of another—wardships of which kind we have hitherto enjoyed by reason of the fee which some one held from us in military service;—and in the matter of abbeys founded in the fee of another than ourselves—in which the lord of the fee may say that he has jurisdiction. And when we return, or if we desist from our pilgrimage, we shall straightway exhibit full justice to those complaining with regard to these matters.

54. No one shall be taken or imprisoned on account of the appeal of a woman concerning the death of another than her husband.

55. All fines imposed by us unjustly and contrary to the law of the land, and all amerciaments made unjustly and contrary to the law of the land, shall be altogether remitted, or it shall be done with regard to them according to the judgment of the twenty five barons mentioned below as sureties for the peace, or according to the judgment of the majority of them together with the aforesaid Stephen archbishop of Canterbury, if he can be present, and with others whom he may wish to associate with himself for this purpose. And if he can not be present, the affair shall nevertheless proceed without him; in such way that, if one or more of the said twenty five barons shall be concerned in a similar com-

pliant, they shall be removed as to this particular decision, and, in their place, for this purpose alone, others shall be substituted who shall be chosen and sworn by the remainder of those twenty five.

56. If we have disseized or dispossessed Welshmen of their lands or liberties or other things without legal judgment of their peers, in England or in Wales,—they shall straightway be restored to them. And if a dispute shall arise concerning this, then action shall be taken upon it in the March through judgment of their peers—concerning English holdings according to the law of England, concerning Welsh holdings according to the law of Wales, concerning holdings in the March according to the law of the March. The Welsh shall do likewise with regard to us and our subjects.

57. But with regard to all those things of which any one of the Welsh was, by king Henry our father or king Richard our brother, disseized or dispossessed without legal judgment of his peers, which we have in our hand or which others hold, and for which we ought to give a guarantee: we shall have respite until the common term for crusaders. Except with regard to those concerning which a plea was moved, or an inquest made by our order, before we took the cross. But when we return from our pilgrimage, or if, by chance, we desist from our pilgrimage, we shall straightway then show full justice regarding them, according to the laws of Wales and the aforesaid districts.

58. We shall straightway return the son of Llewelin and all the Welsh hostages, and the charters delivered to us as surety for the peace.

59. We shall act towards Alexander king of the Scots regarding the restoration of his sisters, and his hostages, and his liberties and his lawful right, as we shall act towards our others barons of England; unless it ought to be otherwise according to the charters which we hold from William, his father, the former king of the Scots. And this shall be done through judgment of his peers in our court.

60. Moreover all the subjects of our realm, clergy as well as laity, shall, as far as pertains to them, observe, with regard

to their vassals, all these aforesaid customs and liberties which we have decreed shall, as far as pertains to us, be observed in our realm with regard to our own.

61. Inasmuch as, for the sake of God, and for the bettering of our realm, and for the more ready healing of the discord which has arisen between us and our barons, we have made all these aforesaid concessions,—wishing them to enjoy for ever entire and firm stability, we make and grant to them the following security: that the barons, namely, may elect at their pleasure twenty five barons from the realm, who ought, with all their strength, to observe, maintain and cause to be observed, the peace and privileges which we have granted to them and confirmed by this our present charter. In such wise, namely, that if we, or our justice, or our bailiffs, or any one of our servants shall have transgressed against any one in any respect, or shall have broken some one of the articles of peace or security, and our transgression shall have been shown to four barons of the aforesaid twenty five: those four barons shall come to us, or, if we are abroad, to our justice, showing to us our error; and they shall ask us to cause that error to be amended without delay. And if we do not amend that error, or, we being abroad, if our justice do not amend it within a term of forty days from the time when it was shown to us or, we being abroad, to our justice: the aforesaid four barons shall refer the matter to the remainder of the twenty five barons, and those twenty five barons, with the whole land in common, shall distrain and oppress us in every way in their power,— namely, by taking our castles, lands and possessions, and in every other way that they can, until amends shall have ben made according to their judgment. Saving the persons of ourselves, our queen and our children. And when amends shall have be made they shall be in accord with us as they had been previously. And whoever of the land wishes to do so, shall swear that in carrying out all the aforesaid measures he will obey the mandates of the aforesaid twenty five barons, and that, with them, he will oppress us to the extent of his power. And, to any one who wishes to do so, we publicly and freely give permission to swear; and we will never prevent any one

from swearing. Moreover, all those in the land who shall be unwilling, themselves and of their own accord, to swear to the twenty five barons as to distraining and oppressing us with them: such ones we shall make to swear by our mandate, as has been said. And if any one of the twenty five barons shall die, or leave the country, or in any other way be prevented from carrying out the aforesaid measures,—the remainder of the aforesaid twenty five barons shall choose another in his place, according to their judgment, who shall be sworn in the same way as the others. Moreover, in all things entrusted to those twenty five barons to be carried out, if those twenty five shall be present and chance to disagree among themselves with regard to some matter, or if some of them, having been summoned, shall be unwilling or unable to be present: that which the majority of those present shall decide or decree shall be considered binding and valid, just as if all the twenty five had consented to it. And the aforesaid twenty five shall swear that they will faithfully observe all the foregoing, and will cause them to be observed to the extent of their power. And we shall obtain nothing from any one, either through ourselves or through another, by which any of those concessions and liberties may be revoked or diminished. And if any such thing shall have been obtained, it shall be vain and invalid, and we shall never make use of it either through ourselves or through another.

62. And we have fully remitted to all, and pardoned, all the ill-will, anger and rancor which have arisen between us and our subjects, clergy and laity, from the time of the struggle. Moreover we have fully remitted to all, clergy and laity, and—as far as pertains to us—have pardoned fully all the transgressions committed, on the occasion of that same struggle, from Easter of the sixteenth year of our reign until the re-establishment of peace. In witness of which, moreover, we have caused to be drawn up for them letters patent of lord Stephen, archbishop of Canterbury, lord Henry, archbishop of Dublin, and the aforesaid bishops and master Pandulf, regarding that surety and the aforesaid concessions.

63. Wherefore we will and firmly decree that the English church shall be free, and that the subjects of our realm shall have and hold all the aforesaid liberties, rights and concessions, duly and in peace, freely and quietly, fully and entirely, for themselves and their heirs, from us and our heirs, in all matters and in all places, forever, as has been said. Moreover it has been sworn, on our part as well as on the part of the barons, that all these above mentioned provisions shall be observed with good faith and without any evil intent. The witness being the above mentioned and many others. Given through our hand, in the plain called Runnimede between Windsor and Stanes, on the fifteenth day of June, in the seventeenth year of our reign.

The penchant for constitution-making, for binding citizens into one body by an expressly written compact, was brought early to these shores. The Pilgrims of the Mayflower did not naturally form a political society, with laws and traditions reaching back "in time out of mind." So they attempted to produce a civil society by explicit agreement: a process in which later immigrants to this country would likewise participate. The Compact explicitly specifies that the "Laws, Ordinances, Acts, Constitutions and Offices" are for the "general good of the Colony"; that is, the government must serve the people. Although, in the case of the Pilgrims, they were also trying to bind and control those few people who were not of the Church and whom they feared would cause trouble.

The Mayflower Compact
(1620)

In the Name of God, Amen.

We, whose names are underwritten, the Loyal Subjects of our dread Sovereign Lord King *James*, by the Grace of God, of *Great Britain, France*, and *Ireland*, King, *Defender of the Faith*, &c.

Having undertaken for the Glory of God, and Advancement of the Christian Faith, and Honor of our King and Country, a Voyage to plant the first colony in the northern Parts of Virginia; Do by these Presents, solemnly and mutually in the Presence of God and one another, covenant and combine ourselves together into a civil Body Politic, for our better Ordering and Preservation, and Furtherance of the Ends aforesaid; and by Virtue hereof to enact, constitute, and frame, such just and equal Laws, Ordinances, Acts, Constitutions and Offices, from time to time, as shall be thought most meet and convenient for the general good of the Colony; unto which we promise all due Submission and Obedience. In WITNESS whereof we have hereunto subscribed our names at *Cape Cod*, the 11th of *November*, in the Reign of our Sovereign Lord King *James of England, France* and *Ireland*, the eighteenth and of *Scotland*, the fifty-fourth. *Anno Domini* 1620.

John Carver
William Bradford
Edward Winslow
William Brewster
Issac Allerton
Myles Standish
John Alden
Samuel Fuller
Christopher Martin
William Mullins
William White
Richard Warren
John Howland
Stephen Hopkins

Edward Tilley
John Tilley
Francis Cooke
Thomas Rogers
Thomas Tinker
John Ridgate
Edward Fuller
John Turner
Francis Eaton
James Chilton
John Craxton
John Billington
Joses Fletcher

Degory Priest
Thomas Williams
Gilbert Winslow
Edmund Margeson
Peter Browne
Richard Britterdge
George Soule
Richard Clarke
Richard Gardiner
John Allerton
Thomas English
Edward Doten
Edward Leister
John Goodman

Charles I and his government, like all governments, needed money and invaded the liberties of citizens. After the King tried to force loans and taxes by various means, all of which were resisted by Parliament, and imprisoned certain citizens without showing cause or allowing bail, the House of Commons put together the Petition of Right, causing it to be read three times in each House. The Petition enumerates the rights that Parliament took to be fundamental to Englishmen and English government, including, besides trial by jury and due process, which are found in Magna Carta, the principle that there could be no taxation without the consent of Parliament and the right not to have soldiers quartered on civilians, among others that would become important for the writers of the Constitution.

The Petition of Right
(1628)

To the King's Most Excellent Majesty

Humbly show unto our Sovereign Lord the King, the Lords Spiritual and Temporal, and Commons in Parliament assembled, that whereas it is declared and enacted by a statue made in the time of the reign of King Edward the First, commonly called *Statutum de tallagio non concedendo*, that no tallage or aid shall be laid or levied by the King or his heirs in this realm, without the good will and assent of the Archbishops, Bishops, Earls, Barons, Knights, Burgesses, and other the freemen of the commonalty of this realm: and by authority of Parliament holden in the five and twentieth year of the reign of King Edward the Third, it is declared and enacted, that from thenceforth no person shall be compelled to make any loans to the King against his will, because such loans were against reason and the franchise of the land; and by other laws of this realm it is provided, that none should be charged by any charge or imposition, called a Benevolence, nor by such like charge: by which, the statues before-mentioned, and other good laws and statutes of this realm, your subjects have inherited this freedom, that they should not be compelled to contribute to any tax, tallage, aid, or other like charge, not set by common consent in Parliament:

II. Yet nevertheless, of late divers commissions directed to sundry Commissioners in several counties, with instructions, have issued, by means whereof your people have been in divers places assembled, and required to lend certain sums of money unto your Majesty, and many of them upon their refusal so to do, have had an oath administered unto them, not warrantable by the laws or statutes of this realm, and have been constrained to become bound to make appearance and give attendance before your Privy Council, and in other places, and others of them have been therefore imprisoned, confined, and sundry other ways molested and disquieted: and divers other charges have been laid and levied upon your people in several counties, by Lords Lieutenants, Deputy Lieutenants, Commissioners for Musters, Justices of Peace and others, by command or direction from your Majesty or your Privy Council, against the laws and free customs of this realm.

III. And where also by the statute called, 'The Great Charter of the Liberties of England,' it is declared and enacted, that no freeman may be taken or imprisoned or be disseised of his freehold or liberties, or his free customs, or be outlawed or exiled, or in any manner destroyed, but by the lawful judgment of his peers, or by the law of the land:

IV. And in the eight and twentieth year of the reign of King Edward the Third, it was declared and enacted by authority of Parliament, that no man of what estate or condition that he be, should be put out of his lands or tenements, nor taken, nor imprisoned, nor disherited, nor put to death, without being brought to answer by due process of law:

V. Nevertheless, against the tenor of the said statutes, and other good laws and statutes of your realm, to that end provided, divers of your subjects have of late been imprisoned without any cause showed, and when for their deliverance they were brought before your Justices, by your Majesty's writs of Habeas Corpus, there to undergo and receive as the Court should order, and their keepers commanded to certify the causes of their detainer; no cause was certified, but that they were detained by your Majesty's special command, signified by the Lords of your Privy Council, and yet were returned back to several prisons, without being charged with anything to which they might make answer according to the law.

VI. And whereas of late great companies of soldiers and mariners have been dispersed into divers counties of the realm, and the inhabitants against their wills have been compelled to receive them into their houses, and there to suffer them to sojourn, against the laws and customs of this realm, and to the great grievance and vexation of the people.

VII. And whereas also by authority of Parliament, in the 25th year of the reign of King Edward the Third, it is declared and enacted, that no man shall be forejudged of life or limb against the form of the Great Charter, and the law of the land; and by the said Great Charter and other laws and statutes of this your realm, no man ought to be adjudged to death, but by the laws established in this your realm, either by the customs of the same realm or by Acts of Parliament: and whereas no offender of what kind soever is exempted from the proceedings to be used, and punishments to be inflicted by the laws and statutes of this your realm; nevertheless of late divers commissions under your Majesty's Great Seal have issued forth, by which certain persons have been assigned and appointed Commissioners with power and authority to proceed within the land, according to the justice of martial law against such soldiers and mariners, or other dissolute persons joining with them, as should commit any murder, robbery, felony, mutiny, or other outrage or misdemeanor whatsoever, and by such summary course and order, as is agreeable to martial law, and is used in armies in time of war, to proceed to the trial and condemnation of such offenders, and them to cause to be executed and put to death according to the law martial:

VIII. By pretext whereof, some of your Majesty's subjects have been by some of the said Commissioners put to death, when and where, if by the laws and statutes of the land they had deserved death, by the same laws and statutes also they might, and by no other ought to have been, adjudged and executed:

IX. And also sundry grievous offenders by color thereof, claiming an exemption, have escaped the punishments due to them by the laws and statutes of this your realm, by reason that divers of your officers and ministers of justice have unjustly refused, or forborne to proceed against such offenders according to the same laws and statutes, upon pretence that the said offenders were punishable only by martial law, and by authority of such commissions as aforesaid; which commissions, and all other of like nature, are wholly and directly contrary to the said laws and statutes of this your realm.

X. They do therefore humbly pray your Most Excellent Majesty, that no man hereafter be compelled to make or yield any gift, loan, benevolence, tax, or such like charge, without common consent by Act of Parliament; and that none be called to make answer, or take such oath, or to give attendance, or be confined, or otherwise molested or disquieted concerning the same, or for refusal thereof; and that no freeman, in any such manner as is before-mentioned, be imprisoned or detained; and that your Majesty will be pleased to remove the said soldiers and mariners, and that your people may not be so burdened in time to come; and that the aforesaid commissions for proceeding by martial law, may be revoked and annulled; and that hereafter no commissions of like nature may issue forth to any person or persons whatsoever, to be executed as aforesaid, lest by color of them any of your Majesty's subjects be destroyed or put to death, contrary to the laws and franchise of the land.

XI. All which they most humbly pray of your Most Excellent Majesty, as their rights and liberties according to the laws and statutes of this realm: and that your Majesty would also vouchsafe to declare, that the awards, doings, and proceedings to the prejudice of your people, in any of the premises, shall not be drawn hereafter into consequence or example: and that your Majesty would be also graciously pleased, for the further comfort and safety of your people, to declare your royal will and pleasure, that in the things aforesaid all your officers and ministers shall serve you, according to the laws and statutes of this realm, as they tender the honor of your Majesty, and the prosperity of this kingdom.

The English Civil Wars resulted in the deposition and death of Charles I, and a void in government. Having deposed and killed the King, where was legitimate government to be found? Out of the political ferment of the Civil Wars came a group of men called the Levellers. They were mostly religious Independents, and thus opposed to an established Church. But they also had views about political and social man. They took as their fundamental premise that the people are sovereign and Parliament governs only by consent. From this came their view of the inalienable rights of the individual, of law having authority by the consent of the people, of universal manhood suffrage, of the origin of government in an original compact and of the idea that the powers of government should be limited by a fundamental law emanating from the people. Although the Agreement was not accepted by Cromwell and the army, the ideas it introduced were eagerly embraced by the American Colonists.

An Agreement of the Free People of England
(1649)

Tendered as a *peace-offering* to this distressed *nation*.

By Lieutenant Colonel *John Lilburne*, master *William Walwyn*, master *Thomas Prince*, and master *Richard Overton*, Prisoners in the *Tower of London*, *May* the 1, 1649.

Matth. 5. verse 9. *Blessed are the Peace-makers for they shall be called the children of God.*

A Preparative to all sorts of people.

If afflictions make men wise, and wisdom direct to happiness, then certainly this Nation is not far from such a degree thereof, as may compare if not far exceed, any part of the world: having for some years by-past, drunk deep of the Cup of misery and sorrow. We bless God our consciences are clear from adding affliction to affliction, having ever labored from the beginning, of our public distractions, to compose and reconcile them: and should esteem it the Crown of all our temporal felicity that yet we might be instrumental in procur-

25

ing the peace and prosperity of this Common-wealth the land of our Nativity.

And therefore according to our promise in our late *Manifestation* of the 14 of *April* 1649, (being persuaded of the necessity and justness thereof) as a *Peace-Offering* to the Free people of this Nation, we tender this ensuing Agreement, not knowing any more effectual means to put a final period to all our fears and troubles.

It is a way of settlement, though at first much startled at by some in high authority; yet according to the nature of truth, it has made its own way into the understanding, and taken root in most men's hearts and affections, so that we have real ground to hope (whatever shall become of us) that our earnest desires and endeavors for good to the people will not altogether be null and frustrate.

The life of all things is in the right use and application, which is not our work only, but every man's conscience must look to itself, and not dream out more seasons and opportunities. And this we trust will satisfy all ingenuous people that we are not such wild, irrational, dangerous Creatures as we have been aspersed to be; This Agreement being the ultimate end and full scope of all our desires and intentions concerning the Government of this Nation, and wherein we shall absolutely rest satisfied and acquiesce; nor did we ever give just cause for any to believe worse of us by any thing either said or done by us, and which would not in the least be doubted, but that men consider not the interest of those that have so unchristian-like made bold with our good names; but we must bear with men of such interests as are opposite to any part of this Agreement, when neither our Savior nor his Apostles innocently could stop such men's mouths whose interests their doctrines and practices did extirpate: And therefore if friends at least would but consider what interest men relate to, while they are telling or whispering their aspersions against us, they would find the reason and save us a great deal of labor in clearing ourselves, it being a remarkable sign of an ill cause when aspersions supply the place of arguments.

We bless God that He has given us time and hearts to bring it to this issue, what further he hath for us to do is yet only known to his wisdom, to whose will and pleasure we shall willingly submit; we have if we look with the eyes of frailty, enemies like the sons of *Anak*, but if with the eyes of faith and confidence in a righteous God and a just cause, we see more with us than against us.

From our causeless captivity in the Tower of *London, May* 1, 1649.

| John Lilburn | William Walwyn |
| Thomas Prince | Richard Overton |

The Agreement itself thus follows.

After the long and tedious prosecution of a most unnatural cruel, homebred war, occasioned by divisions and distempers among ourselves, and those distempers arising from the uncertainty of our government, and the exercise of an unlimited or arbitrary power, by such as have been trusted with supreme and subordinate authority, whereby multitudes of grievances and intolerable oppressions have been brought upon us. And finding after eight year's experience and expectation all endeavors hitherto used, or remedies hitherto applied, to have increased rather than diminished our distractions, and that if not speedily prevented our falling again into factions and divisions, will not only deprive us of the benefit of all those wonderful victories God has vouchsafed against such as sought our bondage, but expose us first to poverty and misery, and then to be destroyed by foreign enemies.

And being earnestly desirous to make a right use of that opportunity God has given us to make this nation free and happy, to reconcile our differences, and beget a perfect amity and friendship once more among us, that we may stand clear in our consciences before Almighty God, as unbiased by any corrupt interest or particular advantages, and manifest to all the world that our endeavors have not proceeded from malice to the persons of any, or enmity against opinions; but in reference to the peace and prosperity of the Common-wealth, and for prevention of like distractions, and removal of all grievances; We the free People of *England*, to whom God hath given hearts, means and opportunity to effect the same, do with submission to His wisdom, in His name, and desiring the equity thereof may be to His praise and glory; Agree to ascertain our government, to abolish all arbitrary power, and to set bounds and limits to our supreme, and all subordinate authority, and remove all known grievances.

And accordingly do declare and publish to all the world, that we are agreed as follows,

I. That the supreme authority of *England* and territories therewith incorporated, shall be and reside henceforward in a Representative of the people consisting of four hundred persons, but no more; in the choice of whom (according to natural right) all men of the age of one and twenty years and upwards (not being servants, or receiving alms, or having served the late King in arms or voluntary contributions) shall have their voices; and be capable of being elected to that supreme trust, those who served the King being disabled for ten years only. All things concerning the distribution of the said four hundred members proportionable to the respective parts of the nation, the several places for election, the manner of giving and taking votes, with all circumstances of like nature, tending to the completing and equal proceedings in elections, as also their salary, is referred to be settled by this present Parliament, in such sort as the next Representative may be in a certain capacity to meet with safety at the time herein expressed: and such circumstances to be made perfect by future Representatives.

II. That two hundred of the four hundred members, and not less, shall be taken and esteemed for a competent Representative; and the major voices present shall be concluding to this nation. The place of the session, and choice of Speaker, with other circumstances of that nature, are referred to the care of this and future Representatives.

III. And to the end all public officers may be certainly accountable, and no factions made to maintain corrupt interests, no officer of any salary forces in army or garrison, nor any treasurer or receiver of public monies, shall (while such) be elected a member for any Representative; and if any lawyer shall at any time be chosen, he shall be incapable of practice as a lawyer, during the whole time of that trust. And for the same reason, and that all persons may be capable of subjection as well as rule.

IV. That no member of the present Parliament shall be capable of being elected of the next Representative, nor any member of any future Representative shall be capable of being chosen for the Representative immediately succeeding: but are free to be chosen, one Representative having intervened: Nor shall any member of any Representative be made either receiver, treasurer, or other officer during that employment.

V. That for avoiding the many dangers and inconveniences apparently arising from the long continuance of the same persons in authority; we agree that this present Parliament shall end the first Wednesday in *August* next 1649, and thenceforth be of no power or authority: and in the meantime shall order and direct the election of a new and equal Representative, according to the true intent of this our Agreement: and so as the next Representative may meet and sit in power and authority as an effectual Representative upon the day following; namely the first Thursday of the same *August*, 1649.

VI. We agree, if the present Parliament shall omit to order such election or meeting of a new Representative; or shall by any means be hindered from performance of that trust:

That in such case, we shall for the next Representative proceed in electing thereof in those places, and according to that manner and number formerly accustomed in the choice of knights and burgesses; observing only the exceptions of such persons from being electors or elected, as are mentioned before in the first, third, and fourth Heads of this Agreement: It being most unreasonable that we should either be kept from new, frequent and successive Representatives, or that the supreme authority should fall into the hands of such as have manifested disaffection to our common freedom, and endeavored the bondage of the nation.

VII. And for preserving the supreme authority from falling into the hands of any whom the people have not, or shall not choose,

We are resolved and agreed (God willing) that a *new Representative* shall be upon the first *Thursday* in *August* next aforesaid: the ordering and disposing of themselves, as to the choice of a Speaker, and the like circumstances, is hereby left to their discretion: But are in the extent and exercise of power to follow the direction and rules of this Agreement; and are hereby authorized and required according to their best judgments, to set rules for future equal distribution, and election of members as is herein intended and enjoined to be done, by the present Parliament.

VIII. And for the preservation of the supreme authority (in all times) entirely in the hands of such persons only as shall be chosen thereunto—we *agree and declare*: That the next and all future Representatives, shall continue in full power for the space of one whole year: and that the people shall of course, choose a Parliament once every year, so as all the members thereof may be in a capacity to meet, and take place of the foregoing Representative: the first *Thursday* in every *August* for ever if God so please; Also (for the same reason) that the next or any future Representative being met, shall continue their session day by day without intermission for four months at least; and after that shall be at liberty to adjourn from two months to two months, as they shall see cause until their year be expired, but shall sit no longer than a year upon pain of treason to every member that shall exceed that time: and in times of adjournment shall not erect a Council of State but refer the managing of affairs in the intervals to a Committee of their own members giving such instructions, and publish them, as shall in no measure contradict this agreement.

IX. And that none henceforth may be ignorant or doubtful concerning the power of the supreme authority, and of the affairs, about which the same is to be conversant and exercised: we agree and declare, that the power of Representatives shall extend without the consent or concurrence of any other person or persons,

1. To the conservation of peace and commerce with foreign nations.

2. To the preservation of those safeguards, and securities of our lives, limbs, liberties, properties, and estates, contained in the Petition of Right, made and enacted in third year of the late King.

3. To the raising of moneys, and generally to all things as shall be evidently conducive to those ends, or to the enlargement of our freedom, redress of grievances, and prosperity of the Commonwealth.

For security whereof, having by woeful experience found the prevalence of corrupt interests powerfully inclining most men once entrusted with authority, to pervert the same to their own domination, and to the prejudice of our peace and liberties, we therefore further agree and declare.

X. That we do not empower or entrust our said representatives to continue in force, or to make any laws, oaths, or covenants, whereby to compel by penalties or otherwise any person to any thing in or about matters of faith, religion or God's worship or to restrain any person from the profession of his faith, or exercise of religion according to his conscience, nothing having caused more distractions, and heart burnings in all ages, than persecution and molestation for matters of conscience in and about religion:

XI. We do not empower them to impress or constrain any person to serve in war by sea or land, every man's conscience being to be satisfied in the justness of that cause wherein he hazards his own life, or may destroy another's.

And for the quieting of all differences, and abolishing of all enmity and rancor, as much as is now possible for us to effect.

XII. We agree, that after the end of this present Parliament, no person shall be questioned for any thing said or done in reference to the late wars, or public differences; otherwise than in pursuance of the determinations of the present Parliament, against such as have adhered to the King against the liberties of the people: And saving that accountants for public monies received, shall remain accountable for the same.

XIII. That all privileges or exemptions of any persons from the laws, or from the ordinary course of legal proceedings, by virtue of any tenure, grant, charter, patent, degree, or birth, or of any place of residence, or refuge, or privilege of Parliament, shall be henceforth void and null; and the like not to be made nor revived again.

XIV. We do not empower them to give judgment upon anyone's person or estate, where no law hath been before provided, nor to give power to any other court or jurisdiction so to do, because where there is no law, there is no transgression, for men or magistrates to take cognisance of; neither do we empower them to intermeddle with the execution of any law whatsoever.

XV. And that we may remove all long settled grievances, and thereby as far as we are able, take away all cause of complaints, and no longer depend upon the uncertain inclination of Parliaments to remove them, nor trouble ourselves or them with petitions after petitions, as has been accustomed, without fruit or benefit; and knowing no cause why any would repine at our removal of them, except such as make advantage by the continuance, or are related to some corrupt interests, which we are not to regard.

We agree and declare,

XVI. That it shall not be in the power of any Representative, to punish, or cause to be punished, any person or persons for refusing to answer to question against themselves in criminal cases.

XVII. That it shall not be in their power, after the end of the next Representative, to continue or constitute any proceedings in law that shall be longer than six months in the final determination of any cause past all appeal, nor to continue the laws or proceedings therein in any other language than English, nor to hinder any person or persons from pleading their own causes, or of making use of whom they please to plead for them.

The reducing of these and other like provisions of this nature in this Agreement provided, and which could not now in all particulars be perfected by us, is intended by us to be the proper works of faithful Representatives.

XVIII. That it shall not be in their power to continue or make any laws to abridge or hinder any person or persons, from trading or merchandising into any place beyond the seas, where any of this nation are free to trade.

XIX. That it shall not be in their power to continue excise or customs upon any sort of food, or any other goods, wares, or commodities, longer than four months after the beginning of the next Representative, being both of them extremly burthensome and oppressive to trade, and so expensive in the receipt, as the monies expended therein (if collected as subsides have been) would extend very far towards defraying the public charges; and forasmuch as all monies to be raised are drawn from the people; such burthensome and chargeable ways, shall never more be revived, nor shall they raise monies by any other ways (after the aforesaid time) but only by an equal rate in the pound upon every real and personal estate in the nation.

XX. That it shall not be in their power to make or continue any law, whereby men's real or personal estates, or any part thereof, shall be exempted from payment of their debts; or to imprison any person for debt of any nature, it being both unchristian in itself, and no advantage to the creditors, and both a reproach and prejudice to the Common-wealth.

XXI. That it shall not be in their power to make or continue any law, for taking away any man's life, except for murder, or other the like heinous offenses destructive to humane society, or for endeavoring by force to destroy this our Agreement, but shall use their uttermost endeavor to appoint punishments equal to offenses: that so men's lives, limbs, liberties, and estates, may not be liable to be taken away upon trivial or slight occasions as they have been; and shall have special care to preserve, all sorts of people from wicked-ness, misery, and beggary: nor shall the estate of any capital offender be confiscated but in cases of treason only; and in all other capital offenses recompense shall be made to the parties damnified, as well out of the estate of the malefactor, as by loss of life, according to the conscience of his jury.

XXII. That it shall not be in their power to continue or make any law, to deprive any person, in case of trials for life, limb, liberty, or estate, from the benefit of witnesses, on his, or their behalf; nor deprive any person of those privileges, and liberties, contained in the *Petition of Right*, made in the third year of the late King *Charles*.

XXIII. That it shall not be in their power to continue the grievance of tithes, longer than to the end of the next Representative; in which time, they shall provide to give reasonable satisfaction to all impropriators: neither shall they force by penalties or otherwise, any person to pay towards the maintenance of any ministers, who out of conscience cannot submit thereunto.

XXIV. That it shall not be in their power to impose ministers upon any the respective parishes, but shall give free liberty to the parishioners of every particular parish, to choose such as themselves shall approve; and upon such terms, and for such reward, as themselves shall be willing to contribute, or shall contract for. Provided, none be choosers but such as are capable of electing Representatives.

XXV. That it shall not be in their power, to continue or make a law, for any other way of judgements, or conviction of life, limb, liberty, or estate, but only by twelve sworn men of the neighborhood; to be chosen in some free way by the people; to be directed before the end of the next Representative, and not picked and imposed, as hitherto in many places they have been.

XXVI. They shall not disable any person from bearing any office in the Common-wealth, for any opinion or practice in religion, excepting such as maintain the Pope's (or other foreign) supremacy.

XXVII. That it shall not be in their power to impose any public officer upon any counties, hundreds, cites, towns, or boroughs; but the people capable by this Agreement to chose

Representatives, shall chose all their public officers that are in any kind to administer the law for their respective places, for one whole year, and no longer, and so from year to year: and this as an especial means to avoid factions, and parties.

And that no person may have just cause to complain, by reason of taking away the excise and customs, we agree,

XXVIII. That the next, and all future Representatives shall exactly keep the public faith, and give full satisfaction, for all securities, debts, arrears or damages, (justly chargeable) out of the public treasury; and shall confirm and make good all just public purchases and contracts that have been, or shall be made; save that the next Representative may confirm or make null in part or in whole, all gifts of lands, monies, offices, or otherwise made by the present Parliament, to any Member of the House of Commons, or to any of the Lords, or to any of the attendants of either of them.

And for as much as nothing threatens greater danger to the Common-wealth, than that the military power should by any means come to be superior to the civil authority.

XXIX. We do declare and agree, that no forces shall be raised, but by the Representatives, for the time being; and in raising thereof, that they exactly observe these rules, namely, that they allot to each particular county, city, town, and borough, the raising, furnishing, agreeing, and paying of a due proportion, according to the whole number to be levied; and shall to the electors of Representatives in each respective place, give free liberty, to nominate and appoint all officers appertaining to regiments, troops, and companies, and to remove them as they shall see cause, reserving to the Representative, the nominating, and appointing only of the general, and all general-officers; and the ordering, regulating, and commanding of them all, upon what service shall seem to them necessary for the safety, peace, and freedom of the Common-wealth.

And in as much as we have found by sad experience, that generally men make little or nothing, to innovate in government, to exceed their time and power in places of trust, to introduce an arbitrary, and tyrannical power, and to overturn all things into anarchy and confusion, where there are no penalties imposed for such destructive crimes and offenses.

XXX. We therefore agree and declare, that it shall not be in the power of any Representative, in any wise, to render up, or give, or take away any part of this Agreement, nor level men's estates, destroy propriety, or make all things in common: And if any Representative shall endeavor, as a Representative, to destroy this Agreement, every Member present in the House, not entering or immediately publishing his dissent, shall incur the pain due for high treason, and be proceeded against accordingly; and if any person or persons, shall by force endeavor or contrive, the destruction thereof, each person so doing, shall likewise be dealt with as in cases of treason.

And if any person shall by force of arms disturb elections of Representatives, he shall incur the penalty of a riot; and if any person not capable of being an elector, or elected, shall intrude themselves among those that are, or any persons shall behave themselves rudely and disorderly, such persons shall be liable to a presentment by a grand inquest and to an indictment upon misdemeanor; and be fined and otherwise punished according to the discretion and verdict of a jury. And all laws made, or that shall be made contrary to any part of this Agreement, are hereby made null and void.

Thus, as becomes a free people, thankful unto God for this blessed opportunity, and desirous to make use thereof to his glory, in taking off every yoke, and removing every burden, in delivering the captive, and setting the oppressed free; we have in all the particular heads forementioned, done as we would be done unto, and as we trust in God will abolish all occasion of offence and discord, and produce the lasting peace and prosperity of this Common wealth: and accordingly do in the sincerity of our hearts and consciences, as in the presence of Almighty God, give clear testimony of our absolute agreement to all and every part thereof by subscribing our hands thereunto. Dated the first day of *May*, in the year of our Lord 1649.

After the fall of Cromwell's government came the restoration of the Stuart monarchy. The Stuarts continued their drive for absolute government vested in the king; and while Charles II pushed Parliament to the limit, James II pushed it beyond. By using his prerogative to establish such laws as he liked, and his dispensing power to void such laws as Parliament had passed that he didn't like, James went a fair way toward getting the law-making power in his hands alone. But in 1688 his subjects rebelled, James fled, and Parliament declared James had abdicated, and that William and Mary, Prince and Princess of Orange, were now the lawful monarchs of England. In so doing they established parliamentary supremacy, for what Parliament had set up, Parliament could pull down. To make clear the terms under which William and Mary ruled, Parliament passed the Bill of Rights in 1689. This Bill contains many articles we've seen before, but it also includes prohibitions on excessive bail, cruel and unusual punishments, and a declaration of the right to bear arms, among others that would find their way into the Constitution.

The Bill of Rights
(1689)

Whereas the lords spiritual and temporal and commons assembled at Westminster lawfully, fully and freely representing all the estates of the people of this realm, did upon the thirteenth day of February in the year of our Lord one thousand six hundred eighty-eight, present unto Their Majesties, then called and known by the names and style of William and Mary, prince and princess of Orange, being present in their proper persons, a certain declaration in writing made by the said lords and commons in the words following, viz.:

Whereas the late king James the Second by the assistance of divers evil counselors, judges and ministers employed by him did endeavor to subvert and extirpate the Protestant religion and the laws and liberties of this kingdom.

By assuming and exercising a power of dispensing with and suspending of laws, and the execution of laws, without consent of parliament.

By committing and prosecuting divers worthy prelates for humbly petitioning to be excused from concurring to the said assumed power.

By issuing and causing to be executed a commission under the great seal for erecting a court, called the court of commissioners for ecclesiastical causes.

By levying money for and to the use of the crown, by pretence of prerogative, for other time and in other manner than the same was granted by parliament.

By raising and keeping a standing army within this kingdom in time of peace, without consent of parliament, and quartering soldiers contrary to law.

By causing several good subjects being Protestants to be disarmed, at the same time when papists were both armed and employed contrary to law.

By violating the freedom of election of members to serve in parliament.

By prosecutions in the court of king's bench for matters and causes cognizable only in parliament, and by divers other arbitrary and illegal courses.

And whereas of late years partial, corrupt and unqualified persons have been returned and served on juries in trials, and particularly divers jurors in trials for high treason, which were not freeholders.

And excessive bail hath been required of persons committed in criminal cases, to elude the benefit of the laws made for the liberty of the subjects.

And excessive fines have been imposed.

And illegal and cruel punishments have been inflicted.

And several grants and promises made of fines and forfeitures before any conviction or judgement against the persons upon whom the same were to be levied.

All which are utterly and directly contrary to the known laws and statutes and freedom of this realm.

And whereas the said late king James the Second having abdicated the government and the throne being thereby vacant, His Highness the prince of Orange (whom it hath pleased Almighty God to make the glorious instrument of delivering this kingdom from popery and arbitrary power) did (by the advice of the lords spiritual and temporal and divers principal persons of the commons) cause letters to be written to the lords spiritual and temporal, being Protestants; and other letters to the several counties, cities, universities, boroughs, and Cinque ports for the choosing of such persons to represent them, as were of right to be sent to parliament, to meet and sit at Westminster upon the two and twentieth day of January in this year one thousand six hundred eighty and eight, in order to such an establishment as that their religion, laws and liberties might not again be in danger of being subverted; upon which letters electors having been accordingly made,

And thereupon the said lords spiritual and temporal and commons pursuant to their respective letters and elections being now assembled in a full and free Representative of this nation, taking into their most serious consideration the best means for attaining the ends aforesaid, do in the first place (as their ancestors in like case have usually done) for the vindicating and asserting their ancient rights and liberties, declare:

That the pretended power of suspending of laws or the execution of laws by regal authority without consent of parliament is illegal.

That the pretended power of dispensing with laws or the execution of laws by regal authority as it hath been assumed and exercised of late is illegal.

That the commission for erecting the late court of commissioners for ecclesiastical causes and all other commissions and courts of like nature are illegal and pernicious.

That the levying money for or to the use of the crown by pretence of prerogative without grant of parliament for a longer time or in other manner than the same is or shall be granted is illegal.

That it is the right of the subjects to petition the king and all commitments and prosecutions for such petitioning are illegal.

That the raising or keeping a standing army within the kingdom in time of peace unless it be with consent of parliament is against the law.

That the subjects which are Protestants may have arms for their defense suitable to their condition and as allowed by law.

The election of members of parliament ought to be free.

The freedom of speech and debates or proceedings in parliament ought not to be impeached or questioned in any court or place out of parliament.

That excessive bail ought not to be required nor excessive fines imposed nor cruel and unusual punishments inflicted.

That jurors ought to be duly impanelled and returned and jurors which pass upon men in trials for high treason ought to be freeholders.

That all grants and promises of fines and forfeitures of particular persons before conviction are illegal and void.

And that for redress of all grievances and for the amending, strengthening and preserving for the laws parliaments ought to be held frequently.

And they do claim, demand and insist upon all and singular the premises as their undoubted rights and liberties and that no declarations, judgments, doings or proceedings to the prejudice of the people in any of the said premises ought in any wise to be drawn hereafter into consequence or example. To which demand of their rights they are particularly encouraged by the declaration of His Highness the prince of Orange as being the only means for obtaining a full redress and remedy therein. Having therefore an entire confidence that His said Highness the prince of Orange will perfect the deliverance so far advanced by him, and will still preserve them from the violation of their rights, which they have here asserted, and from all other attempts upon their religion, rights and liberties, the said lords spiritual and temporal and commons assembled at Westminster do resolve, that William and Mary, prince and princess of Orange, be and be declared king and queen of England, France and Ireland and the dominions thereunto belonging, to hold the crown and royal dignity of the said kingdoms and dominions to them the said prince and princess during their lives and the life of the survivor of them; and that the sole and full exercise of the regal power be only in and executed by the said prince of Orange in the names of the said prince and princess during their joint lives; and after their deceases the said crown and royal dignity of the said kingdoms and dominions to be to the heirs of the body of the said princess; and for default of such issue to the princess Anne of Denmark and the heirs of her body; and for default of such issue to the heirs of the body of the said prince of Orange. And the lords spiritual and temporal and commons do pray the said prince and princess to accept the same accordingly. And that the oaths thereafter mentioned to be taken by all persons of whom the oaths of allegiance and supremacy might be require by law instead of them; and that the said oaths of allegiance and supremacy be abrogated.

"I, A.B., do sincerely promise and swear, that I will be faithful and bear true allegiance to Their Majesties King William and Queen Mary."

"I, A.B., do swear, that I do from my heart abhor, detest and abjure as impious and heretical this damnable doctrine and position, that princes excommunicated or deprived by the pope or any authority of the see of Rome may be deposed or murdered by their subjects or any other whatsoever. And I do declare that no foreign prince, person, prelate, state or potentate has or ought to have any jurisdiction, power, superiority, preeminence or authority, ecclesiastical or spiritual, within this realm. So help me God."

Upon which Their said Majesties did accept the crown and royal dignity of the kingdoms of England, France and Ireland and the dominions thereunto belonging, according to the resolution and desire of the said lords and commons, contained in the said declaration. And thereupon Their Majesties were pleased, that the said lords spiritual and temporal and commons being the two houses of parliament should continue to sit, and with Their Majesties' royal concurrence make effectual provision for the settlement of the religion, laws and liberties of this kingdom, so that the same for the future might not be in danger again of being subverted, to which the lords spiritual and temporal and commons did agree and proceed to act accordingly. Now in pursuance of the premises, the lords spiritual and temporal and commons in parliament assembled, for the ratifying, confirming and establishing the said declaration and articles, clauses, matters and things therein contained, by the force of a law made in due form by authority of parliament, do pray that it may be declared and enacted, that all and singular the rights and liberties asserted and claimed in the said declaration are the true, ancient and indubitable rights and liberties of the people of this kingdom, and so shall be esteemed, allowed, adjudged, deemed and taken to be, and that all and every the particulars aforesaid shall be firmly and strictly holden and observed, as they are expressed in the said declaration; and all officers and ministers whatsoever shall serve Their Majesties and their successors according to the same in all times to come. And the said lords spiritual and temporal and commons, seriously considering how it hath pleased Almighty God in His marvelous providence and merciful goodness to this nation to provide and preserve Their said Majesties' royal persons and most happily to reign over us upon the throne of their ancestors, for which they render unto Him from the bottom of their hearts their humblest thanks and praises, do truly, firmly, assuredly and in the sincerity of their heats think, and do hereby humbly recognize, acknowledge and declare, that King James the Second having abdicated the government and Their Majesties having accepted the crown and the royal dignity aforesaid, Their majesties did become, were, are and of right ought to be by the laws of this realm our sovereign liege lord and lady, king and queen of England, France and Ireland and the dominions thereunto belonging, in and to whose princely persons the royal state, crown and dignity of the said realms, with all honors, styles, titles, regalities, prerogatives, powers, jurisdictions and authorities to the same belonging and appertaining, are most fully, rightfully and entirely invested and incorporated, united and annexed; and for preventing all questions and divisions in this realm by reason of any pretended titles to the crown and for preserving a certainty in the succession thereof, in and upon which the unity, peace, tranquillity and safety of this nation doth under God wholly consist and depend, the said lords spiritual and temporal and the commons do beseech Their

Majesties, that it may be enacted, established and declared, that the crown and regal government of the said kingdom and dominions, with all and singular the premises thereunto belonging and appertaining, shall be and continue to Their said Majesties and the survivor of them during their lives and the life of the survivor of them; and that the entire, perfect and full exercise of the regal power and government be only in and executed by His Majesty, in the names of both Their Majesties, during their joint lives; and after their deceases the said crown and premises shall be and remain to the heirs of the body of her Majesty; and for default of such issue to Her Royal Highness the princess Anne of Denmark and the heirs of her body; and for default of such issue to the heirs of the body of His said Majesty; and thereunto the said lords spiritual and temporal and commons do in the name of all the people aforesaid most humbly and faithfully submit themselves, their heirs and posterities forever; and do faithfully promise that they will stand to, maintain and defend Their said Majesties, and also the limitation and succession of the crown herein specified and contained, to the utmost of their powers with their lives and estates against all persons whatsoever that shall attempt anything to the contrary. And whereas it hath been found by experience, that it is inconsistent with the safety and welfare of this Protestant kingdom to be governed by a popish prince or by any king or queen marrying a papist, the said lords spiritual and temporal and commons do further pray, that it may be enacted, that all and every person and persons that is, are or shall be reconciled to or shall hold communion with the See or Church of Rome, or shall profess the popish religion, or shall marry a papist, shall be excluded and be forever incapable to inherit, possess or enjoy the crown and government of this realm and Ireland and the dominions thereunto belonging, or any part of the same, or to have, use or exercise any regal power, authority or jurisdiction within the same; and in all and every such case or cases the people of these realms shall be and are hereby absolved of their allegiance; and the said crown and government shall from time to time descend to and be enjoyed by such person or persons, being Protestants, as should have inherited and enjoyed the same, in case the said person or persons so reconciled, holding communion, or professing, or marrying, as aforesaid, were naturally dead; and that every king and queen of this realm, who at any time hereafter shall come to and succeed in the imperial crown of this kingdom, shall on the first day of the meeting of the first parliament, next after his or her coming to the crown, sitting in his or her throne in the house of peers, in the presence of the lords and commons therein assembled, or at his or her coronation, before such person or persons who shall administer the coronation oath to him or her at the time of his or her taking the said oath, (which shall first happen), make, subscribe and audibly repeat the declaration mentioned in the statute made in the thirtieth year of the reign of King Charles the Second, entitled, An Act for the more effectual preserving of the King's Person and Government, by disabling Papists from sitting in either House of Parliament; but if it shall happen that such king or queen upon his or her succession to the crown of this realm shall be under the age of twelve years, then every such king or queen shall make, subscribe and audibly repeat the said declaration at his or her coronation, or the first day of the meeting of the first parliament as aforesaid, which shall first happen after such king or queen shall have attained the said age of twelve years. All which Their Majesties are contented and pleased shall be declared, enacted and established by authority of this present parliament, and shall stand, remain and be the law of this realm forever; and the same are by Their said Majesties, by and with the advice and consent of the lords spiritual and temporal and commons in parliament assembled, and by the authority of the same, declared, enacted and established accordingly.

II. And be it further declared and enacted by the authority aforesaid, that, from and after this present session of parliament, no dispensation by *non obstante* of or to any statute or any part thereof shall be allowed, but that the same shall be held void and of no effect, except a dispensation be allowed of in such statute, and except in such case as shall be specially provided for by one or more bill or bills to be passed during this present session of parliament.

III. Provided that no charter or grant or pardon, granted before the three and twentieth day of October in the year of our Lord one thousand six hundred and eighty-nine, shall be any ways impeached or invalidated by this act, but that the same shall be and remain of the same force and effect in law and no other than as if this act had never been made.

In 1765 the British government, like all governments, needed more revenue, and Parliament passed the Stamp Act to help raise it. The American Colonists were quick to protest. They took it as a principle of English law, which they got from the great English jurist Edward Coke, who was instrumental in passing the Petition of Right of 1628, that any law against Magna Carta and the rights of Englishmen was void. The Colonists complained on several grounds, the principal of which was that it was an undoubted right of Englishmen that there should be "no taxation without representation." Additionally, they reaffirmed their rights to trial by jury (affirmed in Magna Carta) and to petition the king (affirmed in the Bill of Rights of 1689). Having seen off an attempt by the Stuart monarchy to set up unlimited power in the Crown, the Colonists were now faced with a Parliament that seemed to claim absolute sovereignty.

Declarations of the Stamp Act Congress

In Congress, at New York, October 19, 1765.

The members of this Congress, sincerely devoted, with the warmest sentiments of affection and duty to His Majesty's person and Government, inviolably attached to the present happy establishment of the Protestant succession, and with minds deeply impressed by a sense of the present and impending misfortunes of the British colonies on this continent; having considered as maturely as time would permit, the circumstances of the said colonies, esteem it our indispensable duty to make the following declarations, of our humble opinion, respecting the most essential rights and liberties of the colonists, and of the grievances under which they labor, by reason of several acts of Parliament.

1st. That His Majesty's subjects in these colonies, owe the same allegiance to the Crown of Great Britain, that is owing from his subjects born within the realm, and all due subordination to that august body, the Parliament of Great Britain.

2nd. That His Majesty's liege subjects in these colonies are entitled to all the inherit rights and privileges of his natural born subjects within the kingdom of Great Britain.

3rd. That it is inseparably essential to the freedom of a people, and the undoubted rights of Englishmen, that no taxes should be imposed on them, but with their own consent, given personally, or by their representatives.

4th. That the people of these colonies are not, and from their local circumstances, cannot be represented in the House of Commons in Great Britain.

5th. That the only representatives of the people of these colonies, are persons chosen therein, by themselves; and that no taxes ever have been, or can be constitutionally imposed on them, but by their respective legislatures.

6th. That all supplies to the Crown, being free gifts of the people, it is unreasonable and inconsistent with the principles and spirit of the British constitution, for the people of Great Britain to grant to His Majesty the property of the colonists.

7th. That trail by jury is the inherent and invaluable right of every British subject in these colonies.

8th. That the late act of Parliament, entitled, "An act for granting and applying certain stamp duties, and other duties in the British colonies and plantations in America, etc.," by imposing taxes on the inhabitants of these colonies, and the said act, and several other acts, by extending the jurisdiction of the courts of admiralty beyond its ancient limits, have a manifest tendency to subvert the rights and liberties of the colonists.

9th. That the duties imposed by several late acts of Parliament, from the peculiar circumstances of these colonies, will be extremely burthensome and grievous, and from the scarcity of specie, the payment of them absolutely impracticable.

10th. That as the profits of the trade of these colonies ultimately center in Great Britain, to pay for the manufactures which they are obliged to take from thence, they eventually contribute very largely to all supplies granted there to the Crown.

11th. That the restrictions imposed by several late acts of Parliament, on the trade of these colonies, will render them unable to purchase the manufactures of Great Britain.

12th. That the increase, prosperity and happiness of these colonies, depend on the full and free enjoyment of their rights and liberties, and an intercourse, with Great Britain, mutually affectionate and advantageous.

13th. That it is the right of the British subjects in these colonies to petition the King or either house of Parliament.

Lastly, that it is the indispensable duty of these colonies to the best of sovereigns, to the mother country, and to themselves, to endeavor by a loyal and dutiful address to His Majesty, and humble application to both houses of Parliament, to procure the repeal of the act granting and applying certain stamp duties, of all clauses of any other acts of Parliament, whereby the jurisdiction of the admiralty is extended as aforesaid, and of the other late acts for the restriction of the American commerce.

When the British Parliament passed the Coercive Acts and made rebellion in the Colonies all but inevitable, the Colonists decided to call a continental congress so that they might present a united front. The Declaration and Resolves of this Congress passed almost without dissent: all but two of the resolutions were passed *Nemine Contradicente* (i.e., without opposition, abbreviated N.C.D. in the text). The Declaration and Resolves put the case as the Colonists understood it on the eve of the Revolution, and is a restatement that the Americans were "entitled to all the rights, liberties, and immunities" of Englishmen. But one novel point occurs in Resolution 10, in which the Colonists assert the necessary separation of the branches of governmental power, as against the unitary power of the British government, and in anticipation of the separation of powers embodied in the Constitution.

Declaration and Resolves of the First Continental Congress

In Congress, at Philadelphia, October 14, 1774.

Whereas, since the close of the last war, the British Parliament, claiming a power of right to bind the people of America, by statute, in all cases whatsoever, hath in some acts expressly imposed taxes on them, and in others, under various pretenses, but in fact for the purpose of raising a revenue, hath imposed rates and duties payable in these colonies, established a board of commissioners, with unconstitutional powers, and extended the jurisdiction of courts of Admiralty, not only for collecting the said duties, but for the trial of causes merely arising within the body of a country.

And whereas, in consequence of other statutes, judges, who before held only estates at will in their offices, have been made dependent on the Crown alone for their salaries, and standing armies kept in times of peace:

And whereas, it has lately been resolved in Parliament, that by force of a statute, made in the thirty-fifth year of the reign of King Henry the Eighth, colonists may be transported to England, and tried there upon accusations for treasons, and misprisions, or concealment of treasons committed in the colonies, and by a late statute, such trials have been directed in cases therein mentioned.

And whereas, in the last session of Parliament, three statutes were made; one, entitled, "An act to discontinue, in such manner and for such time as are therein mentioned, the landing and discharging, lading, or shipping of goods, wares and merchandise, at the town, and within the harbor of Boston, in the province of Massachusetts Bay, in North America"; another, entitled "An act for the better regulating the government of the province of the Massachusetts Bay in New England"; and another, entitled "An act for the impartial administration of justice, in the cases of persons questioned for any act done by them in the execution of the law, or for the suppression of riots and tumults, in the province of the Massachusetts Bay, in New England." And another statute was then made, "for making more effectual provision for the government of the province of Quebec, etc." All which statutes are impolitic, unjust and cruel, as well as unconstitutional, and most dangerous and destructive of American rights.

And whereas, assemblies have been frequently dissolved, contrary to the rights of the people, when they attempted to deliberate on grievances; and their dutiful, humble, loyal, and reasonable petitions to the Crown for redress, have been repeatedly treated with contempt by His Majesty's ministers of state:

The good people of the several colonies of New Hampshire, Massachusetts Bay, Rhode Island and Providence Plantations, Connecticut, New York, New Jersey, Pennsylvania, New Castle, Kent and Sussex on Delaware, Maryland, Virginia, North Carolina, and South Carolina, justly alarmed at these arbitrary proceedings of Parliament and administration, have severally elected, constituted, and appointed deputies to meed and sit in general congress, in the city of Philadelphia, in order to obtain such establishment, as that their religion, laws, and liberties may not be subverted:

Whereupon the deputies so appointed being now assembled, in a full and free representation of these colonies, taking into their most serious consideration, the best means of attaining the ends aforesaid, do, in the first place, as Englishmen, their ancestors in likes cases have usually done, for asserting and vindicating their rights and liberties, declare,

That the inhabitants of the English colonies in North America, by the immutable laws of nature, and principles of the English Constitution, and the several charters or compacts, have the following rights:

Resolved, N.C.D. 1. That they are entitled to life, liberty, and property, and they have never ceded to any sovereign power whatever, a right to dispose of either without their consent.

Resolved, N.C.D. 2. That our ancestors, who first settled these colonies, were at the time of their emigration from the mother country, entitled to all the rights, liberties, and immunities of free and natural-born subjects, within the realm of England.

Resolved, N.C.D. 3. That by such emigration they by no means forfeited, surrendered, or lost any of those rights, but that they were, and their descendants now are, entitled to the exercise and enjoyment of all such of them, as their local and other circumstances enable them to exercise and enjoy.

Resolved, 4. That the foundation of English liberty, and of all free government, is a right in the people to participate in their legislative council: and as the English colonists are not represented, and from their local and other circumstances, can not properly be represented in the British Parliament, they are entitled to a free and exclusive power of legislation in their several provincial legislatures, where their right of representation can alone be preserved, in all cases of taxation and internal polity, subject only to the negative of their sovereign, in such manner as had been theretofore used and accustomed. But, from the necessity of the case, and a regard to the mutual interest of both countries, we cheerfully consent to the operation of such acts of the British Parliament, as are bona fide, restrained to the regulation of our external commerce, for the purpose of securing the commercial advantages of the whole empire to the mother country, and the commercial benefits of its respective members; excluding every idea of taxation, internal or external, for raising a revenue on the subjects in America, without their consent.

Resolved, N.C.D. 5. That the respective colonies are entitled to the common law of England, and more especially to the great and inestimable privilege of being tried by their peers of the vicinage, according to the course of that law.

Resolved, 6. That they are entitled to the benefit of such of the English statutes as existed at the time of their colonization; and which they have, by experience, respectively found to be applicable to their several local and other circumstances.

Resolved, N.C.D. 7. That these, His Majesty's colonies, are likewise entitled to all the immunities and privileges granted and confirmed to them by royal charters, or secured by their several codes of provincial laws.

Resolved, N.C.D. 8. That they have a right peaceably to assemble, consider of their grievances, and petition the King; and that all prosecutions, prohibitory proclamations, and commitments for the same, are illegal.

Resolved, N.C.D. 9. That the keeping a standing army in these colonies, in times of peace, without the consent of the legislature of that colony, in which such army is kept, is against the law.

Resolved, N.C.D. 10. It is indispensably necessary to good government, and rendered essential by the English constitution, that the constituent branches of the legislature be independent of each other; that, therefore, the exercise of legislative power in several colonies, by a council appointed, during pleasure by the Crown, is unconstitutional, dangerous, and destructive to the freedom of American legislation.

All and each of which the aforesaid deputies, in behalf of themselves and their constituents, do claim, demand, and insist on, as their indubitable rights and liberties; which can not be legally taken from them, altered or abridged by any power whatever, without their own consent, by their representatives in their several provincial legislatures.

In the course of our inquiry, we find many infringements and violations of the foregoing rights, which, from an ardent desire, that harmony and mutual intercourse of affection and interest may be restored, we pass over for the present, and proceed to state such acts and measures as have been adopted since the last war, which demonstrate a system formed to enslave America.

Resolved, N.C.D. That the following acts of Parliament are infringements and violations of the rights of the colonists; and that the repeal of them is essentially necessary in order to restore harmony between Great Britain and the American colonies, viz.;

The several acts of 4 Geo. 3. ch.15, and ch. 34.—5 Geo. 3. ch. 25.—6 Geo. 3. ch. 52.—7 Geo. 3. ch. 41, and ch. 46.—8 Geo. 3. ch. 22, which impose duties for the purpose of raising a revenue in America, extend the powers of the admiralty courts beyond their ancient limits, deprive the American subject of trial by jury, authorize the judges' certificate to indemnify the prosecutor for damages, that he might otherwise be liable to, requiring oppressive security from a claimant of ships and goods seized, before he shall be allowed to defend his property, and are subversive of American rights.

Also the 12 Geo. 3. ch. 24, entitled "An act for the better securing His Majesty's dock-yards, magazines, ships, ammunition, and stores," which declares a new offence in America, and deprives the American subject of a constitutional trial by jury of the vicinage, by authorizing the trial of any person, charged with committing any offense described in the said act, out of the realm, to be indicted and tried for the same in any shire or county with the realm.

Also the three acts passed in the last session of Parliament, for stopping the port and blocking up the harbor of Boston, for altering the charter and government of the Massachusetts Bay, and that which is entitled "An act for the better administration of justice," etc.

Also the act passed in the same session for establishing the Roman Catholic religion in the province of Quebec, abolishing the equitable system of English laws, and erecting a tyranny there, to the great danger, from so total a dissimilarity of religion, law, and government of the neighboring British colonies, by the assistance of whose blood and treasure the said country was conquered from France.

Also the act passed in the same session for the better providing suitable quarters for officers and soldiers in His Majesty's service in North America.

Also, that the keeping a standing army in several of these colonies in time of peace, without the consent of the legislature of that colony in which such army is kept, is against the law.

To these grievous acts and measures, Americans can not submit, but in hopes that their fellow subjects in Great Britain will, on a revision of them, restore us to that state in which both countries found happiness and prosperity, we have for the present only resolved to pursue the following peaceable measures:

1st. To enter into a non-importation, non-consumption, and non-exportation agreement or association.

2. To prepare an address to the people of Great Britain, and a memorial to the inhabitants of British America, and

3. To prepare a loyal address to His Majesty; agreeable to resolutions already entered into.

When revolution became inevitable, the Colonists decided to publish their case to the world (and especially to France, from whom they hoped for assistance). The Declaration itself consists of three parts. The first contains the glorious ringing phrases of the first three paragraphs outlining the premise of the argument: that government is founded upon the consent of the governed, the social compact that has played such an important role in Anglo-American political thinking and that goes right back to Magna Carta, and which was made explicit in the Agreement of the People. The second part is a long list of grievances intending to show that the British government had violated the compact, a list of violations many of which have been seen before in these documents. And the third part is the last paragraph declaring the independence of the Colonies.

The Declaration of Independence
(1776)

The Unanimous Declaration of the Thirteen United States of America.

When, in the course of human events, it becomes necessary for one people to dissolve the political bands which have connected them another, and to assume, among the powers of the earth, the separate and equal station to which the laws of nature and of nature's God entitle them, a decent respect to the opinions of mankind requires that they should declare the causes which impel them to the separation.

We hold these truths to be self-evident: that all men are created equal; that they are endowed, by their Creator, with certain unalienable rights; that among these rights are life, liberty, and the pursuit of happiness. That to secure these rights, governments are instituted among men, deriving their just powers from the consent of the governed; that whenever any form of government becomes destructive of these ends, it is the right of the people to alter or abolish it, and to institute new government, laying its foundation on such principles, and organizing its powers in such form, as to them shall seem most likely to effect their safety and happiness. Prudence, indeed, will dictate, that governments long established, should not be changed for light and transient causes; and accordingly all experience hath shown, that mankind are more disposed to suffer, while evils are sufferable, than to right themselves by abolishing the forms to which they are accustomed. But when a long train of abuses and usurpations, pursuing invariably the same object, evinces a design to reduce them under absolute despotism, it is their right, it is their duty, to throw off such government, and to provide new guards for their future security. Such has been the patient sufferance of these colonies; and such is now the necessity which constrains them to alter their former systems of government. The history of the present King of Great Britain is a history of repeated injuries and usurpations, all having in direct object the establishment of an absolute tyranny over these states. To prove this, let facts be submitted to a candid world.

He has refused his assent to laws the most wholesome and necessary for the public good.

He has forbidden his governors to pass laws of immediate and pressing importance, unless suspended in their operation till his assent should be obtained; and when so suspended, he has utterly neglected to attend to them.

He has refused to pass other laws for the accommodation of large districts of people, unless those people would relinquish the right of representation in the legislature; a right inestimable to them, and formidable to tyrants only.

He has called together legislative bodies at places unusual, uncomfortable, and distant from the depository of public records, for the sole purpose of fatiguing them into compliance with his measures.

He has dissolved representative houses repeatedly, for opposing, with manly firmness, his invasions on the rights of the people.

He has refused for a long time, after such dissolutions, to cause others to be elected; thereby the legislative powers, incapable of annihilation, have returned to the people at large for their exercise; the state remaining, in the mean time, exposed to all the dangers of invasion from without, and convulsions within.

He has endeavored to prevent the population of these States; for that purpose obstructing the laws for naturalization of foreigners; refusing to pass others to encourage their migration hither, and raising the conditions of new appropriations of lands.

He has obstructed the administration of justice, by refusing his assent to laws for establishing judiciary powers.

He has made judges dependent on his will alone, for the tenure of their offices, and the amount and payment of their salaries.

He has erected a multitude of new offices, and sent hither swarms of officers to harass our people, and eat out their substance.

He has kept among us, in times of peace, standing armies, without the consent of our legislatures.

He has affected to render the military independent of, and superior to, the civil power.

He has combined with others to subject us to a jurisdiction foreign to our constitution, and unacknowledged by our laws; giving his assent to their acts of pretended legislation:

For quartering large bodies of armed troops among us;

For protecting them, by a mock trial, from punishment for any murders which they should commit on the inhabitants of these states;

For cutting off our trade with all parts of the world;

For imposing taxes on us without our consent;

For depriving us, in may cases, of the benefits of trial by jury;

For transporting us beyond the seas to be tried for pretended offenses;

For abolishing the free system of English laws in a neighboring province, establishing therein an arbitrary government, and enlarging its boundaries, so as to render it at once an example and fit instrument for introducing the same absolute rule into these colonies;

For taking away our charters, abolishing our most valuable laws, and altering fundamentally the forms of our governments;

For suspending our own legislatures, and declaring themselves invested with power to legislate for us in all cases whatsoever.

He has abdicated government here, by declaring us out of his protection, and waging war against us.

He has plundered our seas, ravaged our coasts, burnt our towns, and destroyed the lives of our people.

He is at this time transporting large armies of foreign mercenaries to complete the works of death, desolation, and tyranny, already begun with circumstances of cruelty and perfidy, scarcely paralleled in the most barbarous ages, and totally unworthy the head of a civilized nation.

He has constrained our fellow-citizens, taken captive on the high seas, to bear arms against their country, to become executioners of their friends and brethren, or to fall themselves by their hands.

He has excited domestic insurrections amongst us, and has endeavored to bring on the inhabitants of our frontiers the merciless Indian savages, whose known rule of warfare is an undistinguished destruction of all ages, sexes and conditions.

In every stage of these oppressions we have petitioned for redress in the most humble terms. Our repeated petitions have been answered only by repeated injury. A prince, whose character is thus marked by every act which may define a tyrant, is unfit to be the ruler of a free people.

Nor have we been wanting in attention to our British brethren. We have warned them, from time to time, of attempts by their legislature to extend an unwarrantable jurisdiction over us. We have reminded them of the circumstances of our emigration and settlement here. We have appealed to their native justice and magnanimity, and we have conjured them by ties of our common kindred to disavow these usurpations, which would inevitably interrupt our connections and correspondence. They too have been deaf to the voice of justice and of consanguinity. We must, therefore, acquiesce in the necessity which denounces our separation, and hold them, as we hold the rest of mankind, enemies in war, in peace friends.

We, therefore, the representatives of the United States of America, in General Congress assembled, appealing to the Supreme Judge of the world for the rectitude of our intentions, do, in the name, and by the authority of the good people of these colonies, solemnly publish and declare, That these United Colonies are, and of right ought to be free and independent States; that they are absolved from all allegiance, to the British crown, and that all political connection between them and the state of Great Britain is, and ought to be, totally dissolved; and that as free and independent States, they have full power to levy war, conclude peace, contract alliances, establish commerce, and to do all other acts and things which independent States may of right do. And for the support of this Declaration, with a firm reliance on the protection of Divine Providence, we mutually pledge to each other our lives, our fortunes, and our sacred honor.

John Hancock

New Hampshire
Josiah Bartlett
Wm. Whipple
Matthew Thornton

Massachusetts Bay
Saml. Adams
John Adams
Robt. Treat Paine
Elbridge Gerry

Rhode Island
Step. Hopkins
William Ellery

Connecticut
Roger Sherman
Sam. Huntington
Wm. Williams
Oliver Wolcott

New York
Wm. Floyd
Phil. Livingston
Frans. Lewis
Lewis Morris

New Jersey
Richd. Stockton
Jno. Witherspoon
Fras. Hopkinson
John Hart
Abra. Clark

Pennsylvania
Robt. Morris
Benjamin Rush
Benja. Franklin
John Morton
Geo. Clymer
Jas. Smith
Geo. Taylor
James Wilson
Geo. Ross

Delaware
Caesar Rodney
Geo. Read
Tho. M'Kean

Maryland
Samuel Chase
Wm. Paca
Thos. Stone

Charles Carroll
of Carrollton

Virginia
George Wythe
Richard Henry Lee
Th Jefferson
Benja. Harrison
Thos. Nelson, Jr.
Francis Lightfoot Lee
Carter Braxton

North Carolina
Wm. Hooper
Joseph Hewes
John Penn

South Carolina
Edward Rutledge
Thos. Heyward, Junr.
Thomas Lynch, Junr.
Arthur Middleton

Georgia
Button Gwinnett
Lyman Hall
Geo. Walton

The Articles of Confederation are something of an oddity among the documents of this collection. They were a compact, not among the people or between the people and the government, but among sovereign states. Article II reads: "Each state retains its sovereignty, freedom and independence, and every power, jurisdiction and right which is not by this Confederation expressly delegated to the United States in Congress assembled." The Articles contain many items we have previously seen, and many more which will appear in the Constitution: extradition of felons fleeing jurisdiction, freedom of speech, limits on a standing army, the power to declare war and peace, to regulate weights and measures, and to establish post offices and borrow money, among others.

Articles of Confederation
(1778)

To all to whom these presents shall come, we the undersigned delegates of the states affixed to our names, send greeting:

Whereas the delegates of the United States of America in Congress assembled, did, on the fifteenth day of November in the year of our Lord seventeen seventy-seven, and in the second year of the Independence of America, agree to Certain Articles of Confederation and perpetual union between the states of New Hampshire, Massachusetts Bay, Rhode Island and Providence Plantations, Connecticut, New York, New Jersey, Pennsylvania, Delaware, Maryland, Virginia, North Carolina, South Carolina and Georgia in the words following, viz.:

Articles of Confederation and Perpetual Union Between the States of New Hampshire, Massachusetts Bay, Rhode Island and Providence Plantations, Connecticut, New York, New Jersey, Pennsylvania, Delaware, Maryland, Virginia, North Carolina, South Carolina and Georgia

ARTICLE I. The style of this Confederacy shall be "The United States of America."

ARTICLE II. Each state retains its sovereignty, freedom and independence, and every power, jurisdiction and right which is not by this Confederation expressly delegated to the United States in Congress assembled.

ARTICLE III. The said states hereby severally enter into a firm league of friendship with each other for their common defense, the security of their liberties, and their mutual and general welfare, binding themselves to assist each other against all force offered to, or attacks made upon them, or any of them, on account of religion, sovereignty, trade, or any other pretense whatever.

ARTICLE IV. The better to secure and perpetuate mutual friendship and intercourse among the people of the different States in the Union, the free inhabitants of each of these states, paupers, vagabonds and fugitives from justice excepted, shall be entitled to all privileges and immunities of free citizens in the several states; and the people of each state shall have free ingress and regress to and from any other state, and shall enjoy therein all the privileges of trade and commerce, subject to the same duties, impositions and restrictions as the inhabitants thereof respectively; provided, that such restrictions shall not extend so far as to prevent the removal of property imported into any state, to any other state of which the owner is an inhabitant; provided also, that no imposition, duties or restriction shall be laid by any state on the property of the United States, or either of them.

If any person guilty of or charged with treason, felony, or other high misdemeanor of any state, shall flee from justice, and be found in any of the United States, he shall upon demand of the governor or executive power of the state from which he fled, be delivered up and removed to the state having jurisdiction of his offense.

Full faith and credit shall be given in each of these states to the records, acts and judicial proceedings of the courts and magistrates of every other state.

ARTICLE V. For the more convenient management of the general interests of the United States, delegates shall be annually appointed in such manner as the legislature of each state shall direct, to meet in Congress on the first Monday in November, in every year, with a power reserved to each state, to recall its delegates, or any of them, at any time within the year, and to send others in their stead, for the remainder of the year.

No state shall be represented in Congress by less than two, nor by more than seven members; and no person shall be capable of being a delegate for more than three years in any term of six years; nor shall any person, being a delegate, be capable of holding any office under the United States, for which he, or another for his benefit receives any salary, fees or emolument of any kind.

Each state shall maintain its own delegates in a meeting of the states, and while they act as members of the committee of the states.

In determining questions in the United States, in Congress assembled, each state shall have one vote.

Freedom of speech and debate in Congress shall not be impeached or questioned in any court, or place out of Congress, and the members of Congress shall be protected in their persons from arrests and imprisonments, during the time of their going to and from, and attendance on Congress, except for treason, felony, or breach of the peace.

ARTICLE VI. No state without the consent of the United States in Congress assembled, shall send any embassy to, or receive any embassy from, or enter into any conference, agreement, alliance or treaty with any king, prince or state; nor shall any person holding any office of profit or trust under the United States, or any of them, accept of any present, emolument, office or title of any kind whatever from any king, prince or foreign state; nor shall the United States in Congress assembled, or any of them, grant any title of nobility.

No two or more states shall enter into any treaty, confederation or alliance whatever between them, without the consent of the United Sates in Congress assembled, specifying accurately the purposes for which the same is to be entered into, and how long it shall continue.

No state shall lay any imposts or duties, which may interfere with any stipulation in treaties, entered into by the United States in Congress assembled, with any king, prince or state, in pursuance of any treaties already proposed by Congress, to the courts of France and Spain.

No vessels of war shall be kept up in time of peace by any state, except such number only as shall be deemed necessary by the United States in Congress assembled, for the defense of such state, or its trade; nor shall any body of forces be kept up by any state, in time of peace, except such number only, as in the judgment of the United States, in Congress assembled, shall be deemed requisite to garrison the forts necessary for the defense of such state; but every state shall always keep up a well regulated and disciplined militia, sufficiently armed and accoutered, and shall provide and constantly have ready for use, in public stores, a due number of field pieces and tents, and a proper quantity of arms, ammunition and camp equipage.

No state shall engage in any war without the consent of the United States in Congress assembled, unless such state be actually invaded by enemies, or shall have received certain advice of a resolution being formed by some nation of Indians to invade such state, and the danger is so imminent as not to admit of a delay, till the United States in Congress assembled can be consulted: nor shall any state grant commissions to any ships or vessels of war, nor letters of marque or reprisal, except it be after a declaration of war by the United States in Congress assembled, and then only against the kingdom or state and the subjects thereof, against which war has been so declared, and under such regulations as shall be established by the United States in Congress assembled, unless such state be infested by pirates, in which case vessels of war may be fitted out for that occasion, and kept so long as the danger shall continue, or until the United Sates in Congress assembled shall determine otherwise.

ARTICLE VII. When land forces are raised by any state for the common defense, all officers of or under the rank of colonel, shall be appointed by the Legislature of each state respectively by whom such forces shall be raised, or in such manner as such state shall direct, and all vacancies shall be filled up by the state which first made the appointment.

ARTICLE VIII. All charges of war, and all other expenses that shall be incurred for the common defense or general welfare, and allowed by the United States in Congress assembled, shall be defrayed out of a common treasury, which shall be supplied by the several states, in proportion to the value of all land within each state, granted to or surveyed for any person, as such land and the buildings and improvements thereon shall be estimated according to such mode as the United States in Congress assembled, shall from time to time direct and appoint.

The taxes for paying that proportion shall be laid and levied by the authority and direction of the legislature of the several states within the time agreed upon by the United States in Congress assembled.

ARTICLE IX. The United States in Congress assembled, shall have the sole and exclusive right and power of determining on peace and war except in the cases mentioned in the sixth article—of sending and receiving ambassadors—entering into treaties and alliances; provided that no treaty of commerce shall be made whereby the legislative power of the respective states shall be restrained from imposing such imposts and duties on foreigners, as their own people are subjected to, or from prohibiting the exportation or importation of any species of goods or commodities whatsoever—of establishing rules for deciding in all cases, what captures on land or water shall be legal, and in what manner prizes taken by land or naval forces in the service of the United States shall be divided or appropriated—of granting letters of marque and reprisal in times of peace—appointing courts for the trial of piracies and felonies committed on the high seas and establishing courts for receiving and determining finally appeals in all cases of captures, provided that no member of Congress shall be appointed a judge of any of the said courts.

The United States in Congress assembled shall also be the last resort on appeal in all disputes and differences now subsisting or that hereafter may arise between two or more states concerning boundary, jurisdiction or any cause whatever; which authority shall always be exercised in the manner following. Whenever the legislative or executive authority or lawful agent of any state in controversy with another shall present a petition to Congress, stating the matter in question and praying for a hearing, notice thereof shall be given by order of Congress to the legislative or executive authority of the other state in controversy, and a day assigned for the appearance of the parties by their lawful agents, who shall then be directed to appoint by joint consent commissioners or judges to constitute a court for hearing and determining the matter in question: but if they can not agree, Congress shall name three persons out of each of the United States, and from the list of such persons each party shall alternately strike out one, the petitioners beginning, until the number shall be reduced to thirteen; and from that number not less than seven, nor more than nine names, as Congress shall direct, shall in the presence of Congress be drawn out by lot, and the persons whose names shall be so drawn or any five of them, shall be commissioners or judges, to hear and finally determine the controversy, so always as a major part of the judges who shall hear the cause shall agree in the determination: and if either party shall neglect to attend at the day appointed, without showing reasons, which Congress shall judge sufficient, or being present shall refuse to strike, the Congress shall proceed to nominate three persons out of each state, and the Secretary of Congress shall strike in behalf of such party absent or refusing; and the judgment and sentence of the court to be appointed, in the manner before prescribed, shall be final and conclusive; and if any of the parties shall refuse to submit to the authority of such court, or to appear or defend their claim or cause, the court shall, nevertheless, proceed to pronounce sentence, or judgment, which shall in like manner be final and decisive, the judgment or sentence and other proceedings being in either case transmitted to Congress, and lodged among the acts of Congress for the security of the parties concerned: provided that every commissioner, before he sits in judgment, shall take an oath to be administered by one of the judges of the supreme or superior court of the state where the cause shall be tried, "well and truly to hear and determine the matter in question, according to the best of his judgment, without favor, affection, or hope of reward": provided also that no state shall be deprived of territory for the benefit of the United States.

All controversies concerning the private right of soil claimed under different grants of two or more states, whose jurisdiction as they may respect such lands, and the states which passed such grants are adjusted, the said grants or either of them being at the same time claimed to have originated antecedent to such settlement of jurisdiction, shall on the petition of either party to the Congress of the United States, be finally determined as near as may be in the same manner as is before prescribed for deciding disputes respecting territorial jurisdiction between different states.

The United States in Congress assembled shall also have the sole and exclusive right and power of regulating the alloy and value of coin struck by their own authority, or by that for the respective states—fixing the standard of weights and measures throughout the United States—regulating the trade, and managing all affairs with the Indians, not members of any of the states, providing that the legislative right of any state within its own limits be not infringed or violated—establishing and regulating post offices from one state to another, throughout all the United States, and exacting such postage on the papers passing through the same as may be requisite to defray the expenses of the said office—appointing all officers of the land forces, in the service of the United States, excepting regimental officers—appointing all the officers of the naval forces, and directing their operations.

The United States in Congress assembled shall have authority to appoint a committee, to sit in the recess of Congress, to be denominated "a Committee of the States," and to consist of one delegate from each state; and to appoint such other committees and civil officers as may be necessary for managing the general affairs of the United States under their direction—to appoint one of their number to preside, provided that no person be allowed to serve in the office of president more than one year in any term of three years; to ascertain the necessary sums of money to be raised for the service of the United States, and to appropriate and apply the same for defraying the public expenses—to borrow money, or emit bills on the credit of the United States, transmitting every half year to the respective states an account of the sums of money so borrowed or emitted—to build and equip a navy—to agree upon the number of land forces, and to make requisitions from each state for its quota, in proportion to the number of white inhabitants in such state; which requisition shall be binding, and thereupon the legislature of each state shall appoint the regimental officers, raise the men and clothe, arm and equip them in a solderlike manner, at the expense of the United States; and the officers and men so clothed, armed and equipped shall march to the place appointed, and within the time agreed on by the United States in Congress assembled: but if the United States in Congress assembled shall, on consideration of circumstances judge proper that any state should not raise men, or should raise a smaller number than its quota, and that any other state should raise a greater number of men than the quota thereof, such extra number shall be raised, officered, clothed, armed and equipped in the same manner as the quota of such state, unless the legislature of such state shall judge that such extra number can not be safely spared out of the same, in which case they shall raise, officer, clothe, arm and equip as many of such extra number as they judge can be safely spared. And the officers and men so clothed, armed, and equipped, shall march to the place appointed, and within the time agreed on by the United States in Congress assembled.

The United States in Congress assembled shall never engage in a war, nor grant letters of marque and reprisal in time of peace, nor enter into any treaties or alliances, nor coin money, nor regulate the value thereof, nor ascertain the sums and expenses necessary for the defense and welfare of the United States, or any of them, nor emit bills, nor borrow money on the credit of the United States, nor appropriate money, nor agree upon the number of vessels of war, to be built or purchased, or the number of land or sea forces to be raised, nor appoint a commander-in-chief of the army or navy, unless nine state assent to the same: nor shall a question on any other point, except for adjourning from day to day be determined, unless by the votes of a majority of the United States in Congress assembled.

The Congress of the United States shall have power to adjourn to any time within the year, and to any place within the United States, so that no period of adjournment be for a longer duration than the space of six months; and shall publish the journal of their proceedings monthly, except such parts thereof relating to treaties, alliances or military operations, as in their judgment require secrecy; and the yeas and nays of the delegates of each state on any question shall be entered on the journal, when it is desired by any delegate; and the delegates of a state, or any of them, at his or their request, shall be furnished with a transcript of the said journal, except such parts as are above excepted, to lay before the legislatures of the several states.

ARTICLE X. The Committee of the States, or any nine of them, shall be authorized to execute, in the recess of Congress, such of the powers of Congress as the United States in Congress assembled, by the consent of nine states, shall from time to time think expedient to vest them with; provided that no power be delegated to the said committee, for the exercise of which, by the Articles of Confederation, the voice of nine states in the Congress of the United States assembled is requisite.

ARTICLE XI. Canada acceding to this Confederation, and joining in the measures of the United States, shall be admitted into, and entitled to all the advantages of this Union: but no other colony shall be admitted into the same, unless such admission be agreed to by nine states.

ARTICLE XII. All bills of credit emitted, moneys borrowed and debts contracted by, or under the authority of Congress, before the assembling of the United States, in pursuance of the present Confederation, shall be deemed and considered as a charge against the United States, for payment and satisfaction whereof the said United States, and the public faith are hereby solemnly pledged.

ARTICLE XIII. Every state shall abide by the determinations of the United States in Congress assembled, on all questions which by this Confederation are submitted to them. And the Articles of this Confederation shall be inviolably observed by every state, and the Union shall be perpetual; nor shall any alteration at any time hereafter be made in any of them, unless such alteration be agreed to in a Congress of the United States, and be afterwards confirmed by the legislatures of every state.

AND WHEREAS it hath pleased the Great Governor of the world to incline the hearts of the legislatures we respectively represent in Congress, to approve of, and to authorize us to ratify the said Articles of Confederation and perpetual Union. Know ye that we the undersigned delegates, by virtue of the power and authority to us given for that purpose, do by these presents, in the name and in behalf of our respective constituents, fully and entirely ratify and confirm each and every of the said Articles of Confederation and perpetual Union, and all and singular the matters and things therein contained: and we do further solemnly plight and engage the faith of our respective constituents, that they shall abide by the determinations of the United States in Congress assembled, on all questions, which by the said Confederation are submitted to them. And that the articles thereof shall be inviolably observed by the states we respectively represent, and that the Union shall be perpetual.

IN WITNESS WHEREOF we have hereunto set our hands in Congress. Done at Philadelphia in the State of Pennsylvania the ninth day of July in the year of our Lord one thousand seven hundred and seventy-eight, and in the third year of the independence of America.

On the part and behalf of the State of New Hampshire.

Josiah Bartlett   John Wentworth, Junr. August 8th 1778

On the part and behalf of the State of Massachsetts Bay.

| John Hancock | Samuel Adams | Elbridge Gerry |
| Francis Dana | James Lovell | Samuel Holton |

On the part and behalf of the State of Rhode Island and Providence Plantations.

William Ellery   Henry Marchant   John Collins

On the part and behalf of the State of Connecticut.

| Roger Sherman | Samuel Huntington | Oliver Wollcott |
| Titus Hosmer | | Andrew Adams |

On the part and behalf of the State of New York.

| Jas. Duane | Fra. Lewis | Wm. Duer |
| | | Gouv. Morris |

On the part and behalf of the State of New Jersey.

Jno. Witherspoon Novr. 26, 1778.   Nathl. Scudder Novr. 26, 1778.

On the part and behalf of the State of Pennsylvania.

| Robt. Morris | Daniel Roberdeau | Jona. Bayard Smith |
| William Clingan | | Joseph Reed 22nd July, 1778 |

On the part and behalf of the State of Deleware.

Tho. M'Kean Feby. 12, 1779 John Dickinson   Nicholas Van Dyke
May 5th, 1779

On the part and behalf of the State of Maryland.

John Hanson March 1, 1781   Daniel Carrol Mar. 1, 1781

On the part and behalf of the State of Virginia.

Richard Henry Lee   John Banister   Thomas Adams
Jno. Harvie   Francis Lightfoot Lee

On the part and behalf of the State of North Carolina.

John Penn July 21st, 1778   Corns. Harnett   Jno. Williams

On the part and behalf of the State of South Carolina.

Henry Laurens   William Henry Drayton   Jno. Mathews
Richd. Hutson   Thos Heyward Junr.

On the part and behalf of the State of Georgia.

Jno. Walton 24th July, 1778   Edwd. Telfair   Edwd. Langworthy

The Constitution represents everything Americans had learned about limiting the powers of government in the 572 years since Magna Carta. Power was carefully circumscribed and divided, not only among the three branches of the Federal government but also between the State and Federal governments. The document, with the exception of the unravelling of the compromise over slavery, served us well for about 150 years. The first sustained assault on the limitations on government came in the 1930s with the New Deal Court's extension of Federal power to control economic activity via the Commerce Clause. Virtually everything done by the Federal government today in setting a minimum wage, setting health and safety requirements, all other economic intervention and much civil rights activity is done under the rubric of the Commerce Clause. The second sustained attack on Constitutional limitations on government came in the 1960s when the Warren Court incorporated the Bill of Rights against the States via the Fourteenth Amendment. This has had the effect of giving the Federal government virtual control over all State activities and rendering federalism, the division of powers between the State and Federal governments, hollow rhetoric, and reducing the Tenth Amendment to a nullity. Once again we are facing a unitary government of extensive powers and a concomitant thirst for revenue. Someone once observed that eternal vigilance is the price of liberty. He wasn't talking about vigilance with respect to external enemies.

Constitution of the United States

In convention, September 17, 1787.

Preamble

We the people of the United States, in order to form a more perfect union, establish justice, insure domestic tranquility, provide for the common defense, promote the general welfare, and secure the blessings of liberty to ourselves and our posterity, do ordain and establish this Constitution for the United States of America.

ARTICLE I

SECTION 1. All legislative powers herein granted shall be vested in a Congress of the United States, which shall consist of a Senate and House of Representatives.

SECTION 2. The House of Representatives shall be composed of members chosen every second year by the people of the several states, and the electors in each state shall have the qualifications requisite for electors of the most numerous branch of the State Legislature.

No person shall be a Representative who shall not have attained to the age of twenty-five years, and been seven years a citizen of the United States, and who shall not, when elected, be an inhabitant of that State in which he shall be chosen.

[Representatives and direct taxes shall be apportioned among the several States which may be included within this Union, according to their respective numbers, which shall be determined by adding to the whole number of free persons, including those bound to service for a term of years, and excluding Indians not taxed, three fifths of all other persons.][1] The actual enumeration shall be made within three years after the first meeting of the Congress of the United States, and within every subsequent term of ten years, in such manner as they shall by law direct. The number of Representatives shall not exceed one for every thirty thousand, but each State shall have at least one Representative; and until such enumeration shall be made, the State of New Hampshire shall be entitled to choose three, Massachusetts eight, Rhode Island and Providence Plantations one, Connecticut five, New York six, New Jersey four, Pennsylvania eight, Delaware one, Maryland six, Virginia ten, North Carolina five, South Carolina five, and Georgia three.

---

1. Changed by section 2 of the 14th Amendment.

When vacancies happen in the representation from any State, the executive authority thereof shall issue writs of election to fill such vacancies.

The House of Representatives shall choose their Speaker and other officers; and shall have the sole power of impeachment.

SECTION 3. The Senate of the United States shall be composed of two Senators from each State, [chosen by the Legislature thereof,][2] for six years; and each Senator shall have one vote.

Immediately after they shall be assembled in consequence of the first election, they shall be divided as equally as may be into three classes. The seats of the Senators of the first class shall be vacated at the expiration of the second year, of the second class at the expiration of the fourth year, and of the third class at the expiration of the sixth year, so that one-third may be chosen every second year; [and if vacancies happen by resignation, or otherwise, during the recess of the Legislature of any State, the executive thereof may make temporary appointments until the next meeting of the Legislature, which shall then fill such vacancies.][3]

No person shall be a Senator who shall not have attained to the age of thirty years, and been nine years a citizen of the United States, and who shall not, when elected, be an inhabitant of that State for which he shall be chosen.

The Vice President of the United States shall be President of the Senate, but shall have no vote, unless they be equally divided.

The Senate shall choose their other officers, and also a President pro tempore, in the absence of the Vice President, or when he shall exercise the office of President of the United States.

The Senate shall have the sole power to try all impeachments. When sitting for that purpose, they shall be on oath or

---

2. Changed by section 1 of the 17th Amendment.
3. Changed by section 2 of the 17th Amendment.

affirmation. When the President of the United States is tried, the Chief Justice shall preside: And no person shall be convicted without the concurrence of two-thirds of the members present.

Judgment in cases of impeachment shall not extend further than to removal from office, and disqualification to hold and enjoy any office of honor, trust or profit under the United States: but the party convicted shall nevertheless be liable and subject to indictment, trail, judgment and punishment, according to law.

SECTION 4. The times, places and manner of holding elections for Senators and Representatives, shall be prescribed in each State by the Legislature thereof; but the Congress may at any time by law make or alter such regulations, except as to the place of choosing Senators.

The Congress shall assemble at least once in every year, and such meeting shall [be on the first Monday in December,][4] unless they shall by law appoint a different day.

SECTION 5. Each House shall be the judge of the elections, returns and qualifications of its own members, and a majority of each shall constitute a quorum to do business; but a smaller number may adjourn from day to day, and may be authorized to compel the attendance of absent members, in such manner, and under such penalties as each House may provide.

Each House may determine the rules of its proceedings, punish its members for disorderly behavior, and, with the concurrence of two-thirds, expel a member.

Each House shall keep a journal of its proceedings, and from time to time publish the same, excepting such parts as may in their judgment require secrecy; and the yeas and nays of the members of either House on any question shall, at the desire of one fifth of those present, be entered on the journal.

Neither House, during the session of Congress, shall, without the consent of the other, adjourn for more than three

---

4. Changed by section 2 of the 20th Amendment.

days, nor to any other place than that in which the two Houses shall be sitting.

SECTION 6. The Senators and Representatives shall receive a compensation for their services, to be ascertained by law, and paid out of the Treasury of the United States. They shall in all cases, except treason, felony and breach of the peace, be privileged from arrest during their attendance at the session of their respective Houses, and in going to and returning from the same; and for any speech or debate in either House, they shall not be questioned in any other place.

No Senator or Representative shall, during the time for which he was elected, be appointed to any civil office under the authority of the United States, which shall have been created, or the emoluments whereof shall have been increased during such time; and no person holding any office under the United States, shall be a member of either House during his continuance in office.

SECTION 7. All bills for raising revenue shall originate in the House of Representatives; but the Senate may propose or concur with amendments as on other bills.

Every bill which shall have passed the House of Representatives and the Senate, shall, before it becomes a law, be presented to the President of the United States; if he approves he shall sign it, but if not he shall return it, with his objections to that House in which it shall have originated, who shall enter the objections at large on their journal, and proceed to reconsider it. If after such reconsideration two-thirds of that House shall agree to pass the bill, it shall be sent, together with the objections, to the other House, by which it shall likewise be reconsidered, and if approved by two-thirds of that House, it shall become a law. But in all such cases the votes of both Houses shall be determined by yeas and nays, and the names of the persons voting for and against the bill shall be entered on the journal of each House respectively. If any bill shall not be returned by the President within ten days (Sundays excepted) after it shall have been presented to him, the same shall be a law, in like manner as if he had signed it, unless the

Congress by their adjournment prevent its return, in which case it shall not be a law.

Every order, resolution, or vote to which the concurrence of the Senate and House of Representatives may be necessary (except on a question of adjournment) shall be presented to the President of the United States; and before the same shall take effect, shall be approved by him, or being disapproved by him, shall be repassed by two-thirds of the Senate and House of Representatives, according to the rules and limitations prescribed in the case of a bill.

SECTION 8. The Congress shall have power to lay and collect taxes, duties, imposts and excises, to pay the debts and provide for the common defence and general welfare of the United States; but all duties, imposts and excises shall be uniform throughout the United States;

To borrow money on credit of the United States;

To regulate commerce with foreign nations, and among the several States, and with the Indian tribes;

To establish an uniform rule of naturalization, and uniform laws on the subject of bankruptcies throughout the United States;

To coin money, regulate the value thereof, and of foreign coin, and fix the standard of weights and measures;

To provide for the punishment of counterfeiting the securities and current coin of the United States;

To establish post offices and post roads;

To promote the progress of science and useful arts, by securing for limited times to authors and inventors the exclusive right to their respective writings and discoveries;

To constitute tribunals inferior to the supreme court;

To define and punish piracies and felonies committed on the high seas, and offenses against the law of nations;

To declare war, grant letters of marque and reprisal, and make rules concerning captures on land and water;

To raise and support armies, but no appropriation of money to that use shall be for a longer term than two years;

To provide and maintain a Navy;

To make rules for the government and regulation of the land and naval forces;

To provide for calling forth the militia to execute the laws of the union, suppress insurrections and repel invasions;

To provide for organizing, arming, and disciplining the militia, and for governing such part of them as may be employed in the service of the United States, reserving to the States respectively, the appointment of the officers, and the authority of training the militia according to the discipline prescribed by Congress;

To exercise exclusive legislation in all cases whatsoever, over such district (not exceeding ten miles square) as may, by cession of particular states, and the acceptance of Congress, become the seat of the government of the United States, and to exercise like authority over all places purchased by the consent of the Legislature of the State in which the same shall be, for the erection of forts, magazines, arsenals, dock-yards, and other needful buildings;—And

To make all laws which shall be necessary and proper for carrying into execution the foregoing powers, and all other powers vested by this Constitution in the Government of the United States, or in any Department or Officer thereof.

SECTION 9. The migration or importation of such persons as any of the States now existing shall think proper to admit, shall not be prohibited by the Congress prior to the year one thousand eight hundred and eight, but a tax or duty may be imposed on such importation, not exceeding ten dollars for each person.

The privilege of the Writ of Habeas Corpus shall not be suspended, unless when in cases of rebellion or invasion the public safety may require it.

No bill of attainder or ex post facto law shall be passed.

No capitation, or other direct, tax shall be laid, unless in proportion to the census or enumeration herein before directed to be taken.[5]

No tax or duty shall be laid on articles exported from any State.

No preference shall be given by any regulation of commerce or revenue to the ports of one State over those of another: nor shall vessels bound to, or from, one State, be obliged to enter, clear, or pay duties in another.

No money shall be drawn from the Treasury, but in consequence of appropriations made by law; and a regular statement and account of receipts and expenditures of all public money shall be published from time to time.

No title of nobility shall be granted by the United States: And no person holding office of profit or trust under them, shall, without the consent of the Congress, accept of any present, emolument, office, or title, of any kind whatever, from any king, prince, or foreign state.

SECTION 10. No State shall enter into any treaty, alliance, or confederation; grant letters of marque and reprisal; coin money; emit bills of credit; make any thing but gold and silver coin a tender in payment of debts; pass any bill of attainder, ex post facto law, or law impairing the obligation of contracts, or grant any title of nobility.

No State shall, without the consent of the Congress, lay any imposts or duties on imports or exports, except what may be absolutely necessary for executing its inspection laws: and the net produce of all duties and imposts, laid by any State on imports or exports, shall be for the use of the Treasury of the United States; and all such laws shall be subject to the revision and control of the Congress.

No State shall, without the consent of the Congress, lay any duty of tonnage, keep troops, or ships of war in time of peace, enter into any agreement or compact with another

---

5. Modified by the 16th Amendment.

State, or with a foreign power, or engage in war, unless actually invaded, or in such imminent danger as will not admit of delay.

Article II

SECTION 1. The executive power shall be vested in a President of the United States of America. He shall hold his office during the term of four years, and, together with the Vice President, chosen for the same term, be elected, as follows.

Each State shall appoint, in such manner as the legislature thereof may direct, a number of electors, equal to the whole number of Senators and Representatives to which the State may be entitled in the Congress: but no Senator or Representative, or person holding an office of trust or profit under the United States, shall be appointed an elector.

[The electors shall meet in their respective States, and vote by ballot for two persons, of whom one at least shall not be an inhabitant of the same State with themselves. And they shall make a list of all the persons voted for, and of the number of votes for each; which list they shall sign and certify, and transmit sealed to the seat of the Government of the United States, directed to the President of the Senate. The President of the Senate shall, in the presence of the Senate and House of Representatives, open all the certificates, and the votes shall be counted. The person having the greatest number of votes shall be the President, if such a number be a majority of the whole number of electors appointed; and if there be more than one who have such majority, and have an equal number of votes, then the House of Representatives shall immediately choose by ballot one of them for President; and if no person have a majority, then from the five highest on the list the said House shall in like manner choose the President. But in choosing the President, the votes shall be taken by States, the representation from each State having one vote; a quorum for this purpose shall consist of a member or members from two-thirds of the States, and a majority of all States shall be necessary to a choice. In every case, after the choice of the President, the person having the greatest number of votes of the electors shall be the Vice President. But if there should remain two or more who have equal votes, the Senate shall choose from them by ballot the Vice President.][6]

The Congress may determine the time of choosing the electors, and the day on which they shall give their votes; which day shall be the same throughout the United States.

No person except a natural born citizen, or a citizen of the United States, at the time of the adoption of this Constitution, shall be eligible to the Office of President; neither shall any person be eligible to that office who shall not have attained to the age of thirty-five years, and been fourteen years a resident within the United States.

[In case of the removal of the President from office, or of his death, resignation, or inability to discharge the powers and duties of the said office, the same shall devolve on the Vice President, and the Congress may by law, provide for the case of removal, death, resignation or inability, both of the President and Vice President, declaring what officer shall then act as President, and such officer shall act accordingly, until the disability be removed, or a President shall be elected.][7]

The President shall, at stated times, receive for his services, a compensation, which shall neither be increased nor diminished during the period for which he shall have been elected, and he shall not receive within that period any other emolument from the United States, or any of them.

Before he enter on the execution of his office, he shall take the following oath or affirmation:—"I do solemnly swear (or affirm) that I will faithfully execute the office of President of the United States, and will to the best of my ability, preserve, protect and defend the Constitution of the United States."

SECTION 2. The President shall be commander-in-chief of the Army and Navy of the United States, and of the militia of the several States, when called into the actual service of the United States; he may require the opinion in writing, of the

---

6. Superseded by the 12th Amendment.
7. Modified by the 25th Amendment.

principal officer in each of the executive departments, upon any subject relating to the duties of their respective offices, and he shall have power to grant reprieves and pardons for offenses against the United States, except in cases of impeachment.

He shall have power, by and with the advice and consent of the Senate, to make treaties, provided two-thirds of the Senators present concur; and he shall nominate, and by and with the advice and consent of the Senate, shall appoint ambassadors, other public ministers and consuls, judges of the Supreme Court, and all other officers of the United States, whose appointments are not herein otherwise provided for, and which shall be established by law: but the Congress may by law vest the appointment of such inferior officers, as they think proper, in the President alone, in the courts of law, or in the heads of departments.

The President shall have power to fill up all vacancies that may happen during the recess of the Senate, by granting commissions which shall expire at the end of the next session.

SECTION 3. He shall from time to time give to the Congress information of the state of the Union, and recommend to their consideration such measures as he shall judge necessary and expedient; he may, on extraordinary occasions, convene both Houses, or either of them, and in case of disagreement between them, with respect to the time of adjournment, he may adjourn them to such time as he shall think proper; he shall receive ambassadors and other public ministers; he shall take care that the laws are faithfully executed, and shall commission all the officers of the United States.

SECTION 4. The President, Vice President and all civil officers of the United States, shall be removed from office on impeachment for, and conviction of, treason, bribery, or other high crimes and misdemeanors.

Article III

SECTION 1. The judicial power of the United States, shall be vested in one Supreme Court, and in such inferior courts as the Congress may from time to time ordain and establish.

The Judges, both of the Supreme and Inferior Courts, shall hold their offices during good behavior, and shall, at stated times, receive for their services, a compensation, which shall not be diminished during their continuance in office.

SECTION 2. The judicial power shall extend to all cases, in law and equity, arising under this Constitution, the laws of the United States, and treaties made, or which shall be made, under their authority;—to all cases affecting ambassadors, or other public ministers and consuls;—to all cases of admiralty and maritime jurisdiction;—to controversies to which the United States shall be a party;—to controversies between two or more States;—between a State and citizens of another State;—between citizens of different States;—between citizens of the same State claiming lands under grants of different States, and between a State, or the citizens thereof, and foreign states, citizens or subjects.[8]

In all cases affecting ambassadors, other public ministers and consuls, and those in which a State shall be party, the Supreme Court shall have original jurisdiction. In all other cases before mentioned, the Supreme Court shall have appellate jurisdiction, both as to law and fact, with such exceptions, and under such regulations as the Congress shall make.

The trial of all crimes, except in cases of impeachment, shall be by jury; and such trial shall be held in the State where the said crimes shall have been committed; but when not committed within any State, the trial shall be at such place or places as the Congress may by law have directed.

SECTION 3. Treason against the United States, shall consist only in levying war against them, or in adhering to their enemies, giving them aid and comfort. No person shall be convicted of treason unless on the testimony of two witnesses to the same overt act, or on confession in open court.

The Congress shall have power to declare the punishment of treason, but no attainder of treason shall work corruption

---

8. But see the 11th Amendment.

of blood, or forfeiture except during the life of the person attainted.

Article IV

SECTION 1. Full faith and credit shall be given in each State to the public acts, records, and judicial proceedings of every other State. And the Congress may by general laws prescribe the manner in which such acts, records and proceedings shall be proved, and the effect thereof.

SECTION 2. The citizens of each State shall be entitled to all privileges and immunities of citizens of the several States.

A person charged in any State with treason, felony, or other crime, who shall flee from justice, and be found in another State, shall on demand of the executive authority of the State from which he fled, be delivered up, to be removed to the State having jurisdiction of the crime.

[No person held to service or labor in one State, under the laws thereof, escaping into another, shall, in consequence of any law or regulation therein, be discharged from such service or labor, but shall be delivered up on claim of the party to whom such service or labor may be due.][9]

SECTION 3. New States may be admitted by the Congress into this Union; but no new State shall be formed or erected within the jurisdiction of any other State; nor any State formed by the junction of two or more States, or parts of States, without the consent of the legislatures of the States concerned as well as of the Congress.

The Congress shall have power to dispose of and make all needful rules and regulations respecting the territory or other property belonging to the United States; and nothing in this Constitution shall be so construed as to prejudice any claims of the United States, or of any particular State.

---

9. Superseded by the 13th Amendment.

SECTION 4. The United States shall guarantee to every State in this Union a republican form of government, and shall protect each of them against invasion; and on application of the Legislature, or the executive (when the Legislature cannot be convened) against domestic violence.

Article V

The Congress, whenever two-thirds of both Houses shall deem it necessary, shall propose amendments to this Constitution, or, on the application of the Legislatures of two-thirds of the several States, shall call a convention for proposing amendments, which, in either case, shall be valid to all intents and purposes, as part of this Constitution, when ratified by the Legislatures of three-fourths of the several States, or by conventions in three-fourths thereof, as the one or the other mode of ratification may be proposed by the Congress: Provided that no amendment which may be made prior to the year one thousand eight hundred and eight shall in any manner affect the first and fourth clauses in the ninth section of the first article; and that no State, without its consent, shall be deprived of its equal suffrage in the Senate.

Article VI

All debts contracted and engagements entered into, before the adoption of this Constitution, shall be as valid against the United States under this Constitution, as under the Confederation.

This Constitution, and the laws of the United States which shall be made in pursuance thereof; and all treaties made, or which shall be made, under the authority of the United States, shall be the supreme law of the land; and the Judges in every State shall be bound thereby, anything in the Constitution or laws of any State to the contrary notwithstanding.

The Senators and Representatives before mentioned, and the members of the several State Legislatures, and all executive and judicial officers, both of the United States and of the several States, shall be bound by oath or affirmation, to support this Constitution; but no religious test shall ever be required as a qualification to any office or public trust under the United States.

Article VII

The ratification of the conventions of nine States, shall be sufficient for the establishment of this Constitution between the States so ratifying the same.

DONE in convention by the unanimous consent of the States present the seventeenth day of September in the year of Our Lord one thousand seven hundred and eighty-seven and of the Independence of the United States of America the twelfth. In witness whereof we have hereunto subscribed our names.

Go: Washington
Presidt and deputy from Virginia

New Hampshire
John Langdon
Nicholas Gilman

Connecticut
Wm Saml Johnson
Roger Sherman

Massachusetts
Nathaniel Gorham
Rufus King

New York
Alexander Hamilton

New Jersey
Wil: Livingston
David Brearley
Wm Paterson
Jona: Dayton

Delaware
Geo: Read
John Dickinson
Jaco: Broom,
Gunning Bedford jun
Richard Bassett

Maryland
James McHenry
Danl Carrol
Dan: of St Thos Jenifer

Pennsylvania
B Franklin
Robt. Morris
Thos FitzSimons
James Wilson
Thomas Mifflin
Geo. Clymer
Jared Ingersoll
Gouv Morris

Virginia
John Blair
James Madison Jr.

North Carolina
Wm Blount
Hu Williamson
Richd Dobbs Spaight

South Carolina
J. Rutledge
Charles Pinckney
Charles Cotesworth
                Pinckney
Pierce Butler

Georgia
William Few
Abr Baldwin

Attest:
William Jackson,
Secretary

Articles in addition to, and amendment of, the Constitution of the United States of America, proposed by Congress, and ratified by the legislatures of the several states, pursuant to Article V of the original Constitution (except Amendment XXI which was ratified by State conventions summoned by Congress). The first ten Amendments were ratified December 15, 1791, and form what is known as the "Bill of Rights."

Amendment I

Congress shall make no law respecting an establishment of religion, or prohibiting the free exercise thereof; or abridging the freedom of speech, or of the press; or the right of the people to peaceably assemble, and to petition the government for a redress of grievances.

Amendment II

A well regulated militia, being necessary to the security of a free State, the right of the people to keep and bear arms, shall not be infringed.

Amendment III

No soldier shall, in time of peace be quartered in any house, without the consent of the owner, nor in time of war, but in a manner to be prescribed by law.

Amendment IV

The right of the people to be secure in their persons, houses, papers, and effects, against unreasonable searches and seizures, shall not be violated, and no warrants shall issue, but upon probable cause, supported by oath or affirmation, and particularly describing the place to be searched, and the persons or things to be seized.

Amendment V

No person shall be held to answer for a capital, or otherwise infamous crime, unless on a presentment or indictment of a grand jury, except in cases arising in the land or naval forces, or in the militia, when in actual service in time of war or public danger; nor shall any person be subject for the same offence to be twice put in jeopardy of life or limb; nor shall be compelled in any criminal case to be a witness against himself, nor be deprived of life, liberty, or property, without due process of law; nor shall private property be taken for public use, without just compensation.

Amendment VI

In all criminal prosecutions, the accused shall enjoy the right to a speedy and public trial, by an impartial jury of the State and district wherein the crime shall have been committed, which district shall have been previously ascertained by law, and to be informed of the nature and cause of the accusation; to be confronted with the witnesses against him; to have compulsory process for obtaining witnesses in his favor, and to have the assistance of counsel for his defense.

Amendment VII

In suits at common law, where the value in controversy shall exceed twenty dollars, the right of trail by jury shall be preserved, and no fact tried by a jury, shall be otherwise reexamined in any court of the United States, than according to the rules of the common law.

Amendment VIII

Excessive bail shall not be required, nor excessive fines imposed, nor cruel and unusual punishments inflicted.

Amendment IX

The enumeration in this Constitution, of certain rights, shall not be construed to deny or disparage others retained by the people.

Amendment X

The powers not delegated to the United States by the Constitution, nor prohibited by it to the States, are reserved to the States respectively, or to the people.

Amendment XI

(Ratified February 7, 1795)

The judicial power of the United States shall not be construed to extend to any suit in law or equity, commenced or prosecuted against one of the United States by citizens of another State, or by citizens or subjects of any foreign state.

Amendment XII

(Ratified July 27, 1804)

The electors shall meet in their respective states and vote by ballot for President and Vice President, one of whom, at least, shall not be an inhabitant of the same state with themselves; they shall name in their ballots the person voted for as President, and in distinct ballots the person voted for as Vice President, and they shall make distinct lists of all persons voted for as President, and of all persons voted for as Vice President, and of the number of votes for each, which lists they shall sign and certify, and transmit to the seat of the government of the United States, directed to the President of the Senate;—The President of the Senate shall, in the presence of the Senate and House of Representatives, open all the certificates and the votes shall then be counted;—The person having the greatest number of votes for President, shall be the President, if such number be a majority of the whole number of electors appointed; and if no person have such majority, then from the persons having the highest numbers not exceeding three on the list of those voted for as President, the House of Representatives shall choose immediately, by ballot, the President. But in choosing the President, the votes shall be taken by States, the representation from each State having one vote; a quorum for this purpose shall consist of a member or members from two-thirds of the States, and a majority of all the States shall be necessary to a choice. [And if the House of Representatives shall not choose a President whenever the right of choice shall devolve upon them, before the fourth day of March next following, then the Vice President shall act as President, as in the case of the death or other constitutional disability of the President.—][10] The person having the greatest number of votes as Vice President, shall be the Vice President, if such number be a majority of the whole number of electors appointed, and if no person have a majority, then from the two highest numbers on the list, the Senate shall chose the Vice President; a quorum for the purpose shall consist of two-thirds of the whole number of Senators, and a majority of the whole number shall be necessary to a choice. But no person constitutionally ineligible to the office of President shall be eligible to that of Vice President of the United States.

Amendment XIII
(Ratified December 6, 1865)

Section 1. Neither slavery nor involuntary servitude, except as a punishment for crime whereof the party shall have been duly convicted, shall exist within the United States, or any place subject to their jurisdiction.

Section 2. Congress shall have the power to enforce this article by appropriate legislation.

Amendment XIV
(Ratified July 9, 1868)

Section 1. All persons born or naturalized in the United States, and subject to the jurisdiction thereof, are citizens of the United States and of the State wherein they reside. No State shall make or enforce any law which shall abridge the privileges or immunities of citizens of the United States; nor

---

10. Superseded by section 3 of the 20th Amendment.

shall any State deprive any person of life, liberty, or property, without due process of law; nor deny to any person within its jurisdiction the equal protection of the laws.

Section 2. Representatives shall be appointed among the several States according to their respective numbers, counting the whole number of persons in each State, excluding Indians not taxed. But when the right to vote at any election for the choice of electors for President and Vice President of the United States, Representatives in Congress, Executive and Judicial officers of a State, or the members of the legislature thereof, is denied to any of the male inhabitants of such State, [being twenty-one years of age,][11] and citizens of the United States, or in any way abridged, except for participation in rebellion, or other crime, the basis of representation therein shall be reduced in the proportion which the number of such male citizens shall bear to the whole number of male citizens twenty-one years of age in such a State.

Section 3. No person shall be a Senator or Representative in Congress, or elector of President and Vice President, or hold any office, civil or military, under the United States, or under any State, who, having previously taken an oath, as a member of Congress, or as an officer of the United States, or as a member of any State Legislature, or as an executive or judicial officer of any State, to support the Constitution of the United States, shall have engaged in insurrection or rebellion against the same, or given aid or comfort to the enemies thereof. But Congress may by a vote of two-thirds of each House, remove such disability.

Section 4. The validity of the public debt of the United States, authorized by law, including debts incurred for payment of pensions and bounties for services in suppressing insurrection or rebellion, shall not be questioned. But neither the United States nor any State shall assume or pay any debt or obligation incurred in aid of insurrection or rebellion against the United States, or any claim for the loss of emanci-

---

11. Changed by section 1 of the 26th Amendment.

pation of any slave; but all such debts, obligations and claims shall be held illegal and void.

Section 5. The Congress shall have power to enforce, by appropriate legislation, the provisions of this article.

Amendment XV
(Ratified February 3, 1870)

Section 1. The right of citizens of the United States to vote shall not be denied or abridged by the United States or by any State on account of race, color, or previous condition of servitude.

Section 2. The Congress shall have power to enforce this article by appropriate legislation.

Amendment XVI
(Ratified February 3, 1913)

The Congress shall have power to lay and collect taxes on incomes, from whatever source derived, without apportionment among the several States, and without regard to any census or enumeration.

Amendment XVII
(Ratified April 8, 1913)

The Senate of the United States shall be composed of two Senators from each State, elected by the people thereof, for six years; and each Senator shall have one vote. The electors in each State shall have the qualifications requisite for electors of the most numerous branch of the State Legislatures.

When vacancies happen in the representation of any State in the Senate, the executive authority of such State shall issue writs of election to fill such vacancies: *Provided*, That the legislature of any State may empower the executive thereof to make temporary appointments until the people fill the vacancies by election as the legislature may direct.

This amendment shall not be so construed as to affect the election or term of any Senator chosen before it becomes valid as part of the Constitution.

Amendment XVIII
(Ratified January 16, 1919)

[Section 1. After one year from the ratification of this article the manufacture, sale, or transportation of intoxicating liquors within, the importation thereof into, or the exportation thereof from the United States and all territory subject to the jurisdiction thereof for beverage purposes is hereby prohibited.

[Section 2. The Congress and the several States shall have concurrent power to enforce this article by appropriate legislation.

[Section 3. This article shall be inoperative unless it shall have been ratified as an amendment to the Constitution by the Legislatures of the several States, as provided in the Constitution, within seven years from the date of the submission hereof to the States by Congress.][12]

Amendment XIX
(Ratified August 18, 1920)

The rights of citizens of the United States to vote shall not be denied or abridged by the United States or by any State on account of sex.

Congress shall have power to enforce this article by appropriate legislation.

---

12. Repealed by section 1 of the 21st Amendment.

Amendment XX
(Ratified January 23, 1933)

Section 1. The terms of the President and Vice President shall end at noon on the 20th day of January, and the terms of Senators and Representatives at noon on the 3d day of January, of the years in which such terms would have ended if this article had not been ratified; and the terms of their successors shall then begin.

Section 2. The Congress shall assemble at least once in every year, and such meeting shall begin at noon on the 3d day of January, unless they shall by law appoint a different day.

Section 3. If, at the time fixed for the beginning of the term of the President, the President elect shall have died, the Vice President elect shall become President. If a President shall not have been chosen before the time fixed for the beginning of his term, or if the President elect shall have failed to qualify, then the Vice President elect shall act as President until a President shall have qualified; and the Congress may by law provide for the case wherein neither a President elect nor a Vice President elect shall have qualified, declaring who shall then act as President, or the manner in which one who is to act shall be selected, and such person shall act accordingly until a President or Vice President shall have qualified.

Section 4. The Congress may by law provide for the case of the death of any of the persons from whom the House of Representatives may choose a President whenever the right of choice shall have devolved upon them, and for the case of the death of any of the persons from whom the Senate may choose a Vice President whenever the right of choice shall have devolved upon them.

Section 5. Sections 1 and 2 shall take effect on the 15th day of October following the ratification of this article.

Section 6. This article shall be inoperative unless it shall have been ratified as an amendment to the Constitution by the Legislatures of three-fourths of the several States within seven years from the date of its submission.

Amendment XXI

(Ratified December 5, 1933)

Section 1. The eighteenth article of amendment to the Constitution of the United States is hereby repealed.

Section 2. The transportation or importation into any State, Territory, or possession of the United States for delivery or use therein of intoxicating liquors, in violation of the laws thereof, is hereby prohibited.

Section 3. This article shall be inoperative unless it shall have been ratified as an amendment to the Constitution by conventions in the several states, as provided in the Constitution, within seven years from the date of the submission hereof to the States by Congress.

Amendment XXII

(Ratified February 27, 1951)

Section 1. No person shall be elected to office of the President more than twice, and no person who had held the office of President, or acted as President, for more than two years of a term to which some other person was elected President shall be elected to the office of the President more than once. But this article shall not apply to any person holding the office of President when this article was proposed by the Congress, and shall not prevent any person who may be holding the office of President, or acting as President, during the term within which this article becomes operative from holding the office of President or acting as President during the remainder of such term.

Section 2. This article shall be inoperative unless it shall have been ratified as an amendment to the Constitution by the legislatures of three-fourths of the several States within seven years from the date of its submission to the States by the Congress.

Amendment XXIII

(Ratified March 29, 1961)

Section 1. The District constituting the seat of Government of the United States shall appoint in such manner as the Congress may direct:

A number of electors of President and Vice President equal to the whole number of Senators and Representatives in Congress to which the District would be entitled if it were a State, but in no event more than the least populous State; they shall be considered, for the purposes of the election of President and Vice President, to be electors appointed by a State; and they shall meet in the District and perform such duties as provided by the twelfth article of amendment.

Section 2. The Congress shall have power to enforce this article by appropriate legislation.

Amendment XXIV

(Ratified January 23, 1964)

Section 1. The right of citizens of the United States to vote in any primary or other election for President or Vice President, for electors for President or Vice President, or for Senator or Representative in Congress, shall not be denied or abridged by the United Sates or any State by reason of failure to pay any poll tax or other tax.

Section 2. The Congress shall have the power to enforce this article by appropriate legislation.

Amendment XXV

(Ratified February 10, 1967)

Section 1. In case of the removal of the President from office or of his death or resignation, the Vice President shall become President.

Section 2. Whenever there is a vacancy in the office of the Vice President, the President shall nominate a Vice President who shall take office upon confirmation by a majority vote of both Houses of Congress.

Section 3. Whenever the President transmits to the President pro tempore of the Senate and the Speaker of the House of Representatives his written declaration that he is unable to discharge the powers and duties of his office, and until he transmits to them a written declaration to the contrary, such powers and duties shall be discharged by the Vice President as Acting President.

Section 4. Whenever the Vice President and a majority of either the principal officers of the executive departments or of such other body as Congress may by law provide, transmit to the President pro tempore of the Senate and the Speaker of the House of Representatives their written declaration that the President is unable to discharge the powers and duties of this office, the Vice President shall immediately assume the powers and duties of the office as Acting President.

Thereafter, when the President transmits to the President pro tempore of the Senate and the Speaker of the House of Representatives his written declaration that no inability exists, he shall resume the powers and duties of his office unless the Vice President and a majority of either the principal officers of the executive department or of such other body as Congress may by law provide, transmit within four days to the President pro tempore of the Senate and the Speaker of the House of Representatives their written declaration that the President is unable to discharge the powers and duties of his office. Thereupon Congress shall decide the issue, assembling within forty-eight hours for that purpose if not in session. If the Congress, within twenty-one days after receipt of the latter written declaration, or, if Congress is not in session, within twenty-one days after Congress is required to assemble, determines by two-thirds vote of both Houses that the President is unable to discharge the powers and duties of his office, the Vice President shall continue to discharge the same as Acting President; otherwise, the President shall resume the powers and duties of his office.

Amendment XXVI
(Ratified July 1, 1971)

Section 1. The right of citizens of the United States, who are eighteen years of age or older, to vote shall not be denied or abridged by the United States or by any State on account of age.

Section 2. The Congress shall have power to enforce this article by appropriate legislation.

Amendment XXVII
(Ratified May 8, 1992)

No law varying the compensation for the services of the Senators and Representatives shall take effect, until an election of Representatives shall have intervened.

Index